OPEN EDUCATION GOES TO CHURCH

Books by Mary Duckert
Published by The Westminster Press

Open Education Goes to Church
Tailor-Made Teaching in the Church School
Help! I Run a Sunday School
Help! I'm a Sunday School Teacher

Open Education Goes to Church

by
MARY DUCKERT

Illustrated by Lee DeGroot

THE WESTMINSTER PRESS
Philadelphia

BOOK DESIGN BY
DOROTHY ALDEN SMITH

Published by The Westminster Press®
Philadelphia, Pennsylvania

PRINTED IN THE UNITED STATES OF AMERICA

Library of Congress Cataloging in Publication Data

Duckert, Mary.
Open education goes to church.

1. Christian education—Teaching methods. 2. Open plan schools. I. Title.
BV1536.5.D8 268′.6 75-45195
ISBN 0-664-24796-2

To Nancy and John Bowe
who have opened church education
to the surprise of teachers
and to the delight of children

Contents

Preface

When I first contemplated writing about open education, I did so because of the letters I had received. Some who had tried it asked for further help, and some had no idea how to begin.

The overwhelming plea was for mass-produced curriculum for openness of several kinds—learning centers for individualized instruction, broadly graded activity center education, and intergenerational experiences.

Encouragement by return mail was not enough. It would literally take a book to answer the questions if, indeed, I could answer them. Appropriate openness is elusive; there are no patterns, only models to vary from. The models are here.

The models did not come from me alone. Even after the book was outlined and roughed out, people who heard I was writing it sent me tales of their adventures in the open classroom. Almost all the profiles in Chapter 5 are from persons who reported their experiences or with whom I worked out learning activities for the special child in the classroom.

One model began over twenty years ago, and I was the

enabler if not the life-giving force. We had a problem room and a problem group for which curriculum materials became another problem. As a director of Christian education, I initiated changes in concert with the teachers. The curriculum adaptations we made were further adapted by the children. We learned as we proceeded that if we did not listen to the voices of aggressive children concerning their learning, they would stop listening to our voices.

We progressed from interest centers to centers of learning, which sometimes took almost the entire hour. The teachers said that they had evolved from clock watchers to clock watchers. Once it had been, "How long, O Lord?" and then it became "How short!"

That kind of church classroom was a rarity in those days, and we all knew it. One day after a planning session I said to a teacher who had for many years taught day school, "We're going to have to call this something."

"Oh, let's not," she said. "Let's just do it and leave it open." We did.

M.D.

Introduction: Get Ready, Get Set, Go!

Open education is already operating in a church somewhere in your area. Teachers in North American churches have heard the word, felt the pressure, needed a change, or copied someone else's program. We hear comments like these:

Christian education committee member: "You want that new kind of education where the kids do whatever they want?"

New minister: "It could be that if we put in open education, our church school would grow again."

Parent new to church: "In Lincoln the twins were in an open classroom and just loved it."

Veteran lead teacher: "I visited over at St. Luke's in their open classroom. Oh, my soul! No schedule. No plan. No leadership. No point. They need to go back to their think stools."

Two seasoned, if not peppery, old writers of interdenominational curriculum materials sparring for first place at a writers' conference: "Open education? Phtt! Don't tell me about that. I taught all eight grades in a one-room schoolhouse," one said. It looked as though she had won.

"I taught in a one-room schoolhouse, too, Della. And it was a *closed* classroom. I'd like to try it again, now that I'm not eighteen years old, inexperienced, and the victim of a shabby teacher preparatory course." You know who reigned at the conference. The open one was queen.

It is hard to tell from what these people have said just what open education means. Is it a plan where learners do whatever they want? Does it increase attendance? Do children love it? Is it without schedule, plan, leadership, and point? Does it resemble what went on in one-room schoolhouses in the 1920's? Sometimes.

We could look at average, conventional classrooms and make sweeping generalizations about them just as these pacesetters have observed open classrooms.

"They sat for a half hour, got up, and went somewhere else and sat for another half hour."

"They don't stand for any monkey business during Bible Hour, and they are packing them in."

"We found our children wanted to go somewhere without a lot of activity and fancy program. That's too much like schoolwork."

"I visited at Oakhurst. Sad. Nothing goes on there. No schedule. No plan. No leadership. No point. Just the same old thing week after week, year after year."

Education is planned, intentional learning. Open education incorporates the learners' choices of how they learn within the system of objectives and observable outcomes.

SEEING AND BELIEVING

It is far easier to discern the reasons for open education and its differences in approach from conventional classroom procedures if you see several examples and forms in action. Unguided observation is not enough orientation, but until you see at least that much, you have no mental picture to modify and to generalize from as you continue learning.

Perhaps the most useful places to visit first are not the churches but the day schools with open classrooms. The reason? It is here that children must learn to read and do math. Therefore, their program must include: (1) objectives, (2) individual assessment, (3) concrete evidence of progress, and (4) plenty of ways and resources available to make progress and satisfy objectives. The room may be noisy, the children may appear to wander from place to place, but if it is an operative open classroom, learning is taking place.

Children may have learned to show visitors their work or guide them through their learning area. Teachers may converse with visitors or not, depending upon their work load and responsibilities for individual progress checks on that day.

When you visit, stay long enough to see more than one phase of the program. It is best if you see the whole moon, but seeing half is helpful.

In one British open classroom of seven- and eight-year-olds the schedule had a rhythm of free choice of work, small-group planning, work choice based on the planning, small-group assessment, free choice of work, etc. A generalization on open classroom structure could not have been made by viewing the first half hour, or any one small segment, for that matter.

When you have seen open education in action, write down your questions about it. Some may be answered as you read about what has been tried in church education. Some may be resolved by visiting in church classrooms and by talking with those persons involved in the classrooms.

The minute you leave the open classroom in the church

and compare it to the day school observation you will realize the futility of generalizing on reasons for being, schedule, plans, and responsibilities of the teachers.

One cannot even generalize on those items from place to place in general education, much less in an open classroom. In a school in Birmingham, England, in conversation with the headmaster, the impression was given that emigrating Sikhs were learning to read at an alarmingly speedy rate compared to those in other schools. The children came to his office now and then to show him their homemade books. He praised them always, but sometimes added, "Much better now, eh?"

On briefly visiting in every classroom in this school built specifically for open education, the observer easily determined that in a given room every homemade book was exactly like every other one, and if it wasn't yet, it would be. Older boys and girls, presumably having outgrown books, wrote long involved sentences over and over again until they were letter and comma perfect. The only openness evident was the design of the school.

THE KEY WORD

Openness is what to look for, strive for, and enjoy once you have found it. It is not a set of plans, a schedule, or a set of resources, though it is reflected in each of these aspects of teaching and learning. It is not just a new way of looking at leadership, though it is partly that. And it is never merely a newly built classroom. Openness is an *attitude* toward teaching and learning. The emphasis in an open classroom is no longer primarily on how we teach but on how children learn.

In an effort to accustom teachers to a new way of looking at their job in the classroom, alternative titles have come into use: "enabler" and "facilitator" are the most common of them. These terms, though often used with the children, are for the teachers' benefit. They are to remind those in charge of the learning how they are to operate. "Teacher" is a neutral title, and children still use and prefer it. For them it doesn't carry the baggage it seems to for the reformer. They don't know about schoolmasters who whacked knuckles with their "pointing sticks" when children whispered for answers, when those knuckles had already been cracked for not knowing the "sums." They have no concept of "teacher" so terrifying that they are not willing to call anyone they like by that title. Enablers and facilitators need not worry about what they are called if as they operate they do indeed enable and facilitate learning.

OPEN EDUCATION GOES TO CHURCH

1 Openness in the Church

Once you have seen what an open classroom looks like in a day school, you can begin to revel in your lot as you plan one in the church. You probably have fewer children and more adults than you saw in the schoolroom. Very likely you have more space, and possibly even a choice of rooms. Your curriculum is far more limited. We need not teach reading and math in the church, though we use the skills the children have already.

But the best news of all is that openness is entirely appropriate to education in the church, because thoughtfulness is at its core. Adults are thoughtful of how children learn. Children are thoughtful in their use of shared resources and in helping the strangers in their midst learn to use them. Children are thoughtful of adults as they wait for the individual attention that they know will come in turn.

When an open classroom fails, always look for thoughtlessness as the cause. Insufficient planning, absent leaders, too few resources changed too seldom, too little participation by the children in the planning, little attention from the church boards for providing adequate space and care of the building can each be part of the reason for collapse.

Thoughtfulness is the expression of our esteem for ourselves and others as human beings. If God's love for his people is the warp of the fabric of our lives together in the church, then our love for others is the weft. Openness becomes part of the content in the classroom rather than a method for getting things done. It is not only a way of life but a state of mind. We bring it to our discussions with the minister and official boards and to our planning with leaders, children, and parents. In the classroom it is evident because it has permeated all our relationships. It is not an easy way of life. It takes energy and concentration to achieve almost anything. Effective thoughtfulness in the open classroom is based in a community of thoughtful people. When one person forgets, another compensates and thus reminds us all.

BEGIN WITH WHY

Always begin with a reason for changing to openness. Write your reason down and read it over. Ask yourself, "If we were to do well what we are doing now, would we need to change?" If the answer is no, ask, "Why aren't we doing well?" List the reasons. Then ask, "Will an open classroom change these factors?" If the answer is still no, are there other valid reasons to change? Perhaps you should seek to do better with what you are doing now. The following are some of the reasons for changing to open education in the church.

TOO FEW IN EACH GRADE

One church in the Midwest had too few children at any grade level from fourth grade through sixth for classes of their own. The Christian education committee suggested combining them into one class. For one wretched year a teacher worked with the class trying to find ways to interest children with so wide a range of abilities, preferences, and attention span. Near the end of the year there was a Scout outing that drew all the boys from class. The teacher was visiting with the few girls remaining.

"Are you going to be our teacher next year?" she was asked.

"I haven't decided, Ruth. I don't think we get much accomplished here," she answered bluntly. "It's hard to find something everyone likes to do."

"Mrs. Jackson," Cathy said, "if you did it like we do it for language arts, we could choose things to do and then we wouldn't always have to do the same thing."

"Yeah," Ruth told her, "we have this little book of assignments we check off, you know? And we make things, and read about them first, and then before that we decide—well, we have these units, you know?"

Mrs. Jackson did *not* know. But she called the girls' teacher and asked to visit during language arts, which turned out to be a broadly graded hour three times a week. The project method was used to satisfy specific objectives written so that boys and girls could understand them. The children were introduced to the units as a group. Living in horse country, they called that "feed bagging" it. The food was the same and each pupil consumed what he or she could. Then they were shown a list of projects, told how long they had to work on them, and approximately how many persons should work on each. It was possible, the teacher said, to do two projects or one, depending on the extent and depth of the planning. The pupils signed up for projects, received approval from the teacher and sometimes realignment of project personnel. Each pupil had an assignment book in which progress and snags were recorded. The teacher met with each small group for assessment sometime during each of the three weekly periods. All units were not organized in the same way. Sometimes the class chose several activities from a long list of independent ones and then one all-class project from two or three projects intended to summarize and reinforce the learning of the units.

The visit to the school was encouraging to Mrs. Jackson. She told the chairman of the Christian education committee that she would like to try a class like that one the next year. (The chairman is quoted at the beginning of this chapter.)

She has just finished her third year of open classroom teaching. She laughs about her first year. "Had I known how *hard* it is, I'd never have started it, but by the time I found out, we all knew how."

Her variety of open education is distinguished by its concrete objectives, participation of the children in planning, and thorough evaluation by them. When asked about any problems with adapting materials she laughed. "The first dismal year I taught conventionally. It's been a song compared to that. If you know what you want to do and you're familiar with the resources, all you need to do is use them your way."

A CHANGING NEIGHBORHOOD

"Some city neighborhoods change from many children to no children," the minister of a large, once-suburban church explained, "but ours changed from an all-white to a racially mixed one."

The white children, new or old in the neighborhood, continued to come to church, but no other color showed up, nor did those children go anywhere else. One of the black officers—a graduate student—told the board that they were going about it all wrong. " 'Welcome' isn't enough, and 'Everybody welcome' is worse," Proctor said. He went out into street ball games, met boys and girls on the way home from school, and spoke to them in the supermarket. Each one was invited to the church on Sunday at ten o'clock. "And don't come alone, hear? It's no fun without a buddy."

On Sunday, Proctor, his wife, and an elderly retired church school teacher met with wry amusement.

"I'm the story man," Proctor announced.

"I'm the drama coach," his wife piped.

"And I fit in any—no, I'll do artwork, and the first project I propose is to paint these walls. Do you—er—think anyone will come?" the former teacher asked.

"We're here," a small voice almost whispered. Two little girls in chubby white coats and holding pocketbooks had sat unnoticed in a corner of the big room. It was a beginning.

Within fifteen minutes thirty-five boys and girls ages six to thirteen were there, and it was well past time to do something. The act-now-plan-later scheme worked the first day largely because of Proctor's bluff and skills with large groups. The children were enthusiastic in their response to singing and story time, and less so to drama, which ended in a blindfold game of identifying persons by their voices.

During the week the three leaders planned for an hour of work center activities from which the boys and girls would choose, and a half hour of story and song. Just short of sixty enthusiasts arrived the next week. They were met with immediate choice. Wandering from drama to art to woodworking to music, they were confused and disappointed. Proctor sensed their dissatisfaction, and immediately called the group together for singing. That was the show they'd come to see—"local stand-up black comedian," Proctor said later. After the story, he explained the work centers. Then he asked, "What kept you from working today?" "We didn't know what to do," one of the older boys said.

"You go there and decide," Proctor told him.

"You mean," the boy persisted, "that if me and my buddy

went to art, we could—well, you know"—he looked up at the ceiling and then circled the walls with his eyes—"paint the walls?"

"Yes!" cheered the retired church school teacher. "Let's paint the walls. Sign up at the art table in ten minutes."

"What if we all wanted to paint the walls?" an older girl asked.

"I don't want to paint, Henrietta," another girl shouted.

"Me neither. I want to be in a pla-a-ay."

The younger children sat and watched soberly. The noisier the older ones got, the quieter the six-, seven-, and eight-year-olds became. The experienced teacher rose. "We have juniors and seniors here, haven't we? Seniors know how to paint and how to be in plays. And juniors don't. Some juniors can't read yet. How many juniors do we have?"

Surprisingly, the "juniors" raised their hands. "Come with me," the woman said. "We'll do some planning of our own."

What developed—miracle of miracles—is today a well-planned, well-run open classroom involving first- through eighth-graders, a core of leaders including the original three, and a substantial number of older youth and adults on a rotating basis working in the centers. The boys and girls tend to stick to one center for the entire work time even after finishing the work. Proctor attributes this to their need for a social rather than an instructional experience. The seniors go from project to project. They painted the dirty room and then gave a Christmas play for the juniors. They ran an emergency clothing drive when an old resident hotel burned to the ground. The juniors do all manner of work at their centers. The room and surrounding corridors are vibrantly decorated with original painting and textured murals. The book tables (there are three) have dog-eared paperback storybooks, and on the wall is a bulletin board with printed reports of Good Books to Read.

While the open classroom has received enthusiastic acclaim from the children and youth of the community, very few parents have joined the church or attended worship.

"The open classroom was not started for that reason," the minister says. "It is enough to know that the boys and girls in the classroom come here and regard themselves as members of our church community. Belonging is touchy business. If their parents are at home elsewhere and we accept that, they may become less reluctant guests when we invite them for their children's 'high holy days.' "

Openness, when it surrounds the open classroom, is a support to that kind of education. Openness in the conception and planning of the classroom brings with it all the inherent dangers of poor or no organization. Had the three leaders not been able to adapt their skills to the events of each of the first few weeks, the results could have been disastrous. This kind of classroom, when observed casually, appears easiest of all models to copy. It is in fact the riskiest. It takes sensitive, strong leaders who are constantly aware of the prevailing winds and instantly willing to steer the clumsy ark in another direction.

GREAT EXPECTATIONS

There are churches with a tradition of sound education. Almost always it is lay people, not professionals, who keep the tradition alive. Where professional church workers are employed, their job is seldom to "do" but to support education. Generally, in such churches the boys and girls attend day schools highly regarded in the community, and their parents are involved in school affairs. There are exceptions. In some communities the churches lead the way and ministers and laity serve as agents of change on school boards and town councils. In either case the educational expectations of the adults for the children are high.

These churches were among the first to strive consciously for open education. Most of them already had a form of openness in their preschool groups. But as the children grew older and grappled with Biblical content the instructional practices resembled more and more the information funnel and less and less those of discovery and invention.

In one church in a downtown area of a city with a sizable suburban population, the church school continues to flourish. For many years it has been a model to neighboring churches. Its programs have been copied without apology.

Open education claimed the interest of the Christian education committee over ten years ago, "and we've made every mistake in the books," the chairman admits. They were victims of their own enthusiasm for educational frontiers when they began. The committee approved the open classroom as a new direction and then began looking for teachers. The recruiters were unable to answer questions from potential teachers. The books, many of them British or about British schools, were not specifically related to church education. Those that were espoused a curriculum used throughout the year in religious education classes in English and Welsh day schools.

One class began in the fall. Fifth- and sixth-graders worked in learning centers with materials adapted by two teachers who by their own admission "barely muddled through by spending all week planning directions and setting up centers." The boys and girls worked like frontiersmen themselves. They knew what was expected of them. By March the teachers were exhausted. They called the class together at the end of a session for evaluating. The discussion was fruitful. Suggestions for next year came with glib candor.

"We need to be together more."

"More kids would come if they didn't have to work so hard."

"We never learn songs anymore."

"The most fun is when we all do something different and put it together to make one thing."

The teachers took the comments seriously. Their planning, preparation, and adapting of materials intended for other methods had been too individualistic. There was no time for the whole group to interact in singing, worship, or just plain self-congratulatory activities after a job is completed and done well.

The next fall they had more times together. The year after that the boys and girls planned with the teachers for "festival Sundays" of worship, song, and display of work. That was the year visitors began coming and the third and fourth grades started an open classroom. The boys and girls became visitors' guides. Evaluation sometimes came at the end of a unit at the instigation of the leaders. More often it occurred during their planning period near the beginning of their seventy-five-minute session.

By now openness is understood and permeates all learning activity. Boys and girls enter the classroom with a tradition of open education and an expectation of more. The entire church school operates in a climate of openness, each classroom with a distinctive style. Only the fifth- and sixth-grade group has one of the original teachers. New leaders with a style partly learned from the former ones and mostly reflecting themselves operate in an ever new educational climate.

One of the first "victims" of the fifth- and sixth-grade group is now a student in the school of education at the state university. She visited the classroom recently and told her old teacher, "We're into learning centers at school, and I thought you invented them!"

OTHER REASONS

Reduced enrollment, a changing neighborhood, and educational expectations are all wholesome reasons for changing an educational program. There are less noble reasons, and where these prevail the innovations sometimes don't get off the ground.

Open education doesn't guarantee increased attendance. It is no surefire way to bring disinterested parents to corporate worship or to add their names to membership rolls. It doesn't solve the problems of teacher recruitment, teacher education, or low institutional morale. Any or all of these things may be an outgrowth of a sturdy system of open education, but none is a legitimate reason for beginning one.

As stated earlier, the emphasis in an open classroom is on how children learn. When the focus shifts to how to use children to modify adult behavior, that is crass exploitation of the children and the school.

Before expending the energy of all those persons needed to change an educational system in your church, examine and reexamine your motives. If you want to succeed, be advised to place your intentions on the side of the learners.

WHO ARE INVOLVED AND HOW

Open classrooms have begun at the instigation of a variety of persons within the church. Sometimes a pastor or a minister of education has set forth a plan and teachers have striven to interpret the design in classroom action. At times parents whose children have experienced openness elsewhere provide the ground swell. But most often it is classroom teachers themselves who want to change *and do not know how to go about it.*

Whoever suggests the innovation is a principal in the action, but all who are responsible for education in the church are implicated.

The minister's chief role is one of support. Support docs not mean smiling on whatever happens and finding out as little about it as possible. Rather, it may mean asking, "What can we do to be of most help to you?" It may mean giving leadership education opportunities, investigating open classrooms elsewhere, and working closely with the leaders as they plan. A pastor in the Northwest *shows* teachers an open classroom by conducting one himself. Pastors are expected to operate within the realm of their proficiencies and to be interested.

The officers need to be informed on the concept of openness when it comes to them as an educational option. Those responsible for the nurture and instruction of children should have the opportunity to discuss styles and purposes of openness with those conversant with them. Sometimes these are representatives of the day schools in the community, teachers and leaders from churches with open classrooms, and area Christian education consultants. If there are workshops in their geographical area, it is as important that officers attend as that they encourage teachers to do so.

Those officers responsible for the use of the building need to be informed of what space is required and how the room will be used. It is best not to have to remove every vestige of the educational enterprise between sessions but accommodation to other programs in the church can be made. Officers will probably not know that setting up work centers, displaying completed work, and involving children in the planning all affect the use of the room. There are ways of short-cutting the time it takes to set up a classroom. There are few effective ways, however, of displaying completed classwork inconspicuously and fewer reasons for it. Children themselves, if given the opportunity, can reduce the problems that often arise concerning use of the room. With one group of sixth-, seventh-, and eighth-graders the question was never "Shall we or shall we not clean up?" but "How can we leave the room in order?"

The custodian, when there is one, *needs instructions and cooperation* from those in charge of the open classroom. What looks like order to a teacher may appear as chaos to unschooled eyes. On the other hand, disorder and filth do not always bother adult leaders as much as they might a custodian. Some open classrooms make garage sales look like model houses on display. It is far easier to keep a room clean if unused furniture and equipment are removed and materials and resources appropriately stored. In one church, children were told not to use the sink in their room because it was full of dirty paintbrushes and paint jars from a weekday event. A busybody fourth-grade girl grimaced, sighed, and set to work. She cleaned the paintbrushes, rinsed off the paint jars, and stacked everything in a corner of the counter in ten minutes. The custodian has reason for displeasure if we refuse to do our share of housekeeping. The child knew enough to save the paint jars; a custodian might think them no longer useful.

The parents and the congregation should be invited to visit the open classroom. Open houses, displays of work done, cassette tapes, and slides showing classroom procedures all help to share the enthusiasm that participants have for their way of educating and learning. Several churches have set up their open house day much as their classrooms are set up. Visitors roam from center to center finding out about the way of working, the content studied, and the fruits of the labor. Older children serve as guides. One small church with an emphasis on family participation has one open classroom for third through sixth grade. On their first open house day there was a balloon center for younger children. Upon receiving their balloons, they ran to the churchyard to play with them, while their parents and older sisters and brothers learned about the new classroom. On the way home in the car a six-year-old said to his participating brother: "Peter, I cannot wait to get into your classroom. You get to give balloons to little kids. I never got to do that in my whole life."

Recruitment committees, from whatever source they come, *need a thorough grounding in the purposes of open education and the responsibilities of those who work in it.* Some of the responsibilities are minor, but some major. Persons recruited should have concern, energy, time, and ability to do group planning. To misrepresent what is involved is thoughtless and may lead to unfortunate misunderstanding among newly recruited teachers as well as those teachers continuing from the previous year.

WHERE TO HOUSE THE CLASSROOM

Open classrooms are found in gymnasiums, dining halls, conventional classrooms, corridors, and any combination of rooms like these. They have even functioned outdoors. There is nothing mystical about the place. Corridor classrooms were a bit of a fad at one time, although their reason for being initially was that there was no better space for great mobility. Old gymnasiums often present an insurmountable acoustical problem, and conventional classrooms are frequently too small. Dining halls are almost always multipurpose rooms and necessitate putting everything away after each session and possibly not being permitted to set up work centers until the last minute. That leaves the outdoors, and no one need remind us of the risks involved there.

To decide on the best place for an open classroom, look at your options, list the advantages and disadvantages, discuss possibilities for adapting the space to your needs, and then decide on the room.

Some factors to consider are:

Can unusable furniture and equipment be removed?
Are there a sufficient number of electrical outlets to accommodate projectors and tape recorders?
Can the room be darkened?

Is water available for artwork and clean up?
Are noisy work centers far enough apart so as not to be distracting to the children as they work?
Are there quiet areas where individuals may do independent research and study?
Is there a space large enough for the entire group to gather?
Is there wall space for the display of written work and artwork?
Is there storage space?

In the open classrooms described in this book, leaders have in every instance accommodated to their physical environment. The more quickly they did so, the sooner they got down to the business of the classroom itself—a place for children to learn. Most of the leaders improved upon their surroundings as time went on, but no one changed them completely except where more children arrived than were expected. They were more concerned with what to put in the classroom than where it was.

WHAT EQUIPMENT DO WE NEED?

In the West, in a colorful, sun-filled room a minister observed an open classroom in action with first- through fourth-graders. He saw an easel and paints, a plant-potting center, a reading table, a choral speaking group, and a corner where two children watched a filmstrip and heard a cassette tape through earphones.

"We could never afford all the equipment," he told his adult guide.

"The only new equipment we bought are the earphones," she told him. "As far as library books go, we have too many duplicates, and we'd be glad to share them with you. In an open classroom we have the sum of the equipment formerly used by individual classes. Sometimes we can't take advantage of all of it. The fifth- and sixth-graders have four sets of wall maps for Old and New Testament studies, and now they need only one. And we have found far less use for chairs. The boys and girls sit on the floor when they sit, and stand for many learning activities."

Equipment, supplies, and resources may be purchased over a long period of time. No one knows precisely what is necessary to the classroom and what is merely handy to have. If you have a tendency to want whatever another group has, don't buy it until you have made a list of everything you want, put everything in order of priority, and found out the prices and total amount. If you still feel you *need* all the items, buy them in the order of their priority as you have the money.

Some churches never had adequate equipment, supplies, and resources for conventional classrooms. Now, with that fact literally in the open, the need for learning aids is acute. One of the first places to look for what you should have had and did not is in a church where they no longer need as much as they once did. Buying used equipment in good condition stretches the funds to be spent on what must be new.

WHAT RESOURCES DO WE NEED?

Some churches have begun and maintained open classrooms without a long-range plan of what is to be accomplished. Most people involved in thriving open classrooms buy and adapt standard church school resources. Most series writers are cognizant of open classrooms even though they do not address themselves exclusively to the leaders of learning center education. Unlike in conventional classroom planning, the materials featuring a number of learning activities are more usable than those with limited options.

Planners look at an objective and then ask themselves, "How can this objective be satisfied through art, story-writing, informal drama, and interviewing?" In conventional classroom planning with its plethora of choices, it is time-consuming just to sort out the one or two things most appropriate for the small group. In planning for openness, the abundance of suggestions is necessary. Resources with well-defined units are easier to work with than those with discrete session plans. Work centers may last anywhere from one session to a whole unit and may grow in popularity as various children complete requirements. Even with popular units, such as the ones on Creation and Christmas, the children are relieved to finish them and go on to a new one with expectancy.

Even with a broadly graded grouping, one age group's resources may appeal to the planners as the year's outline to follow. With an outline of units established, learning activities may be selected on related subjects from resources within the series belonging to other age groups. Most art activities are adaptable to various age groups and talents. Composing original stories may be done through either writing or dictating. Informal dramatization may be spontaneous and different each time or as structured as a puppet play with a plot and lines that remain the same through many performances.

HOW DO WE KNOW IF IT IS WORKING?

The best way to find out how children react to the open classroom is to ask them at the end of a unit. Ask them for suggestions of what to keep and what to add. Discuss their ideas even if at first they seem unrealistic so that they see that adults in the church can accept some of their ideas and discard others.

If you have set objectives and related them to learning

activities with tangible, observable results, you will know what the boys and girls are capable of doing. If you ask as you look at displayed work, "Which of the things you finished are you proudest of, Joanne?" the girl can actually point to the work or refer to a dramatic endeavor, service project, or service of worship. Steer clear of questions related to teaching and concentrate on learning. Many boys and girls are accustomed to being served their education without having anything to say about the menu. In their criticism of it, they begin with "Why don't you . . . ?" Your job in evaluation is to help them learn to say "Why don't we . . . ?" instead.

The open classroom has to go well with the teachers to survive. If two or three leaders work well together, planning gets easier, though it is still time-consuming, and results are more gratifying. Persons thoughtful of one another learn new and better ways of cooperating. During the first year, at least, they do get very tired. Fatigue is not a sign of failure but mortality. In March or April, take it easy. Plan a field trip with other adults along with you as supervisors. Go on a picnic. Cooperate with other groups for an Accomplishment Festival, where the congregation is invited to wander through the church school, ask questions, and observe the kinds of work that can be displayed. These events are a lot of work too, but other people share the load and they don't require as much individual follow-through as unit planning does.

In the chapters that follow, examples of the principles set forth in this chapter are manifested more than once. Many teachers have open classrooms and they approach planning, life in the classroom, and evaluation in a variety of ways. These are designs that have worked and continue to work. They are worth examining. We needn't look at the failures. We already know the end to their stories. Your invention is more likely to run smoothly if your research is done on a working model.

2 Learning Center Model

The learning center model is probably the easiest to adapt as an innovation in a conventional classroom, because its goals and objectives are precise. It requires effort and time on the part of the teachers, but they are rewarded by seeing results in the work of the children.

In the church where this model is operative, each class, consisting of two grades, is housed in a small room and is most manageable when attendance is between eighteen and twenty-five. Centers have small shag rugs on which the children sit. Directions, assignments, and some resources are in boxes at each center. Books that are to be used in several centers are elsewhere in the room. The supply cupboard is the only piece of furniture in the room used by the fifth- and sixth-graders.

The teachers initiate activity and respond to suggestions from the pupils. In the first-and-second-grade classroom, the teachers help the children choose a center in which to work, and they stay nearby in order to help. In the third-and-fourth-grade room, the teachers are available to work in the centers. The fifth- and sixth-graders choose their work, show their contract to a teacher, get it approved, and go about completing the assignments.

A room in another part of the church serves as a resource center with books, pictures, maps, filmstrips, records, projectors, tape recorders, and earphones. It is used by individuals and small groups and is supervised by a librarian. Teachers of young children accompany them to the resource center. Older children transact business with the librarian by themselves.

The goal of the learning center classrooms is to master a body of content by individual pupils so that they equip themselves to react to as well as hear and read Scripture.

The objectives in each classroom are appropriate to the age group but relate as well to the ultimate goal. The descriptions that follow begin with the plan for the fifth- and sixth-graders and show how the plans for the two younger groups relate to it.

FIFTH AND SIXTH GRADES

The schedule is uncomplicated. When a child enters the room around 9:30 A.M. on a Sunday, the choice of work begins. If there is to be an assembly, the teachers inform the pupils as to the time and purpose. Assemblies for planning are generally at 9:50, for review or for evaluation at 10:30. The session is over at 10:45.

The children are highly motivated, and the teachers' expectations for them are equally high. They talk together about concepts, assignments, and contracts with the ease normally reserved for telling a friend about a movie or swapping baseball cards.

A *contract* shows the learners the range of assignments they have to choose from. It helps them plan their time during a unit, and it shows the teachers which assignments are never chosen. Here is an example of a contract. It can be adapted to any unit.

LEARNING CENTER CONTRACT

Name ________________________________

Date ________________________________

1. Pick a Tape
   The tape I will listen to is:
2. Pick a Picture
   The picture I will study is:
3. Pick a Song
   The song I will learn is:
4. Pick a Work Sheet
   I will complete ______ work sheets.
   The titles are:
5. Pick a Person
   The person I picked is:
6. Pick a Word
   The words I picked are:
7. Pick a Place
   The places I picked are:
8. Pick a Puzzle
   I will finish ______ puzzles.
   I will make ______ puzzles.
9. Pick a Story
   The story I will listen to is:
   The story I will read is:
10. Pick a Game
    The game I picked is:

11. Bible Skills
    I am learning to:

To be completed by ____________________
(date)

Signed by ____________________
(pupil)

____
(teacher)

Each pupil keeps his or her contract up to date. Teachers check with each child every week. When assignments require the work of a small group, the boys and girls sometimes organize themselves. Most often a teacher helps them organize.

Every assignment has an observable outcome requiring writing, acting, reporting, singing, or working in an art medium. An *assignment sheet* begins with a concept (love, anger, compassion) and ends with a short statement of what the learner should be able to do. The assignment is in between.

Here is an example of the assignment sheet for "Pick a Picture" (item 2 in the contract).

Assignment Sheet

AUTHORITY

Pick a Picture

1. Choose pictures in magazines and newspapers of people you think have authority.

2. Write down what they have the authority to do and who gave it to them.
3. If another pupil is at this center, compare your pictures and writing with the other person's.
4. List three things Jesus had authority to do. The Scripture references on the sheet in the box will help you.
5. Report on one of the Scripture references by completing one of these projects:
   a. Write an article for the church newspaper.
   b. Draw a cartoon strip.
   c. Make a mural with another person.

Supplies and Resources: Magazines and newspapers, scissors, your notebook and a pencil, a sheet of Scripture references, your Bible.

You should be able to show what you have done in step 5 and tell the rest of us what authority Jesus had and where it came from.

Every unit has a time for reporting, showing, and sharing, but it is not necessarily a long performance. When a whole course is finished, the group invites the congregation to examine the work in a large parlor near the sanctuary. Explanatory cards indicate why each assignment was completed.

Resource materials are nationally produced and organized by units. The teachers make the assignment sheets from the concepts listed in the unit plans and the learning activities suggested in the teacher's guide and pupil's books.

The boys and girls evaluate with the teachers near the end of a unit. Their suggestions are taken seriously. They discuss what they liked and did not like and why. Because of pupils' evaluation, for example, recorded stories are fifteen minutes in length rather than thirty.

THIRD AND FOURTH GRADES

Assignments and contracts are a bit more relaxed with these "middle-aged" elementary children than with the fifth- and sixth-graders. The assignments are on printed cards at each center, and the lead teacher keeps a chart of their completed work which they show or report to the teacher. Assignments may be done by individuals or small groups. The boys and girls generally need adult help at one time or another during the work time.

A visual representation of the work to be done by the whole class and the choices open is sometimes organized on a tic-tac-toe form. Each assignment may be tacked to one of the nine squares and the specified number of pupils sign up for each square until all are assigned.

One unit called "Who Is This Man?" consisted of two parts, one on learning from art and one on learning from Scripture. The intent of the learning from art was twofold: (1) to find out something about what the boys and girls already knew and thought about Jesus and (2) to discover how observant and responsive they were to five traditional art masterpieces about Jesus. Four copies of each painting were cut from the children's books. The masterpieces were *Adoration of the Kings*, by Velázquez; *The Calling of the Apostles Peter and Andrew*, by Duccio; *Christ at the Sea of Galilee*, by Tintoretto; *Christ Healing the Sick*, by Rembrandt; and *Storm on the Sea of Galilee*, by Rembrandt.

The tic-tac-toe grid was on the floor in the middle of the room. Everyone started by selecting a print, which had questions attached, and groups were formed according to the print each chose.

WHO IS THIS MAN?

Learning from Art

TIC	TAC	TOE
Pick a picture. Find the others who have the same print. Discuss the questions attached.	Pose a picture on the same subject. Use no works or movement.	Write a story or poem about the picture. Find a person in the picture to write about.
Draw, paint, or sculpt your own picture on the same subject.	Act out the picture's story.	Make one poster for bulletin board display about your group's picture.
Arrange an original art exhibit with any other group.	Interview the adult class in the kitchen about the picture. Use your study questions.	Contribute something to the class newspaper or television show.

Each of five groups of at least four persons completed the picture study. Then the group chose two activities from the tic-tac-toe form: one to do together and one to do alone or with one other person. No attempt was made to prevent duplication of choices, and though suggestions were made of untried activities, everyone was given free choice. *The only option that was not open was to do nothing.* Everyone ended with a contribution to the class newspaper or television show—now-and-then, off-and-on projects in the class.

For the Learning from Scripture part of the unit, Scriptural background was also assigned from a tic-tac-toe chart. This time, groups of two or three children chose a square to work on, put an X over it, and wrote their names on it. The chart contained nine assignments, and when each assignment was done by two or three children, as many as twenty-seven pupils were accommodated. The boys and girls were told that when they heard the xylophone, they had five more minutes before reporting to the group. They were to tell the story of what they read.

WHO IS THIS MAN?

Learning from Scripture

TIC	TAC	TOE
Read aloud Matthew 2: 1–12. Jesus as a baby. A long story, but a good one.	Read aloud Mark 4: 35–41. Jesus stilling the storm.	Read aloud Mark 6: 1–6. Jesus in the synagogue.
Read aloud Mark 1: 14–20. Jesus choosing his disciples.	Read aloud Mark 5: 35–43. Jesus performing a miracle of healing.	Read aloud Mark 10: 13–16. Jesus inviting children to him.
Read aloud Luke 6: 6–11. Jesus healing on the Sabbath.	Read aloud Matthew 26:20–29. Jesus at the Last Supper.	Read aloud Luke 24: 28–35. The resurrection. Hard to report on but worth it.

When the group assembled, the pupils listened as each small group reported. After each report, the whole group agreed on one or two main ideas to summarize each of the stories. The stories were put in order of birth, work, and resurrection. The summary was saved for the class newspaper.

Use of Art and Music

Every session does not include a tic-tac-toe form. On some days art and music centers are set up before the children arrive. They are invited to use the materials at each center in a cooperative venture responding to what they have learned. Most of the time is spent in the centers planning and creating. A short period of showing and sharing comes at the conclusion of the session. Such a schedule satisfied both the teachers and the children who complained of never having enough time to finish any significant projects requiring paints, clay, concentration, experimentation, and group planning. To refresh their memories on these art and music days, original written work, summary statements, and new words printed on paper strips are posted around the work centers.

Use of Games

Near the end of a unit or course of study, games of review are made and played. The games are generally variations on familiar games. Originally, the board games came with curriculum materials, but as they wore out they were replaced by those made by adults and children. With the same format and rules the content of a game can be changed to fit the unit of study.

One game of footprints tracing the journey of the Ark of the Covenant used first with younger children was revamped by some fourth-graders during a summer unit on Paul. It was played somewhat like parcheesi. The same general game is now played to review the journey of the Hebrews from Egypt to Canaan. (Making these games is of far greater value than playing them because of the research required. Playing familiarizes the children with the names of people and places as well as events in sequence.)

Here are some of the basic games. Each has as its objective *review* of what was already studied. New material is not introduced, although it is possible for a person to play who is unfamiliar with the content if his fellow players are familiar with it. Should you try to adapt any of these games, enlist the help of two or three of the boys and girls in the classes for whom they are intended to ensure their value as review.

WHO AM I?

Two players and one moderator play the game. The moderator has a stack of 3″ x 5″ cards with written profiles of persons from The Acts, chs. 2 to 9. The players have pencils and sheets of paper. When the moderator reads a card, the two players write down the name of the person described. The moderator asks to see the two answers. If both players have the right answer, there is no score. If one player has the correct answer, the other player scores a point. The player with the *highest* score loses. The Scripture reference is given on each card, in case the moderator's answer is challenged.

The following are examples of cards:

I am one of the twelve disciples of Jesus. At Pentecost I preached to the people and told them that God raised Jesus from the dead. Many people believed me and were baptized. (Acts 2:14, 32, 41.)

I was healed by a disciple of Jesus Christ. I asked him for money. He gave me something far better. (Acts 3:1–8.)

I was stoned to death after I preached to the people. Even as I lay dying I asked God to forgive them for what they were doing. (Acts 7:59–60.)

I was an enemy of the people who believed in the resurrection of Jesus Christ. Then I had an experience on the way to Damascus that turned my actions around completely. I became a missionary for Christ. (Acts 8:3; 9:3–4, 20.)

MIX AND MATCH

This table game was originally played to acquaint the children with the Sacraments and acts of worship. As adapted by the boys and girls and a teacher it was used as a table game to teach how work gets done in the church and by whom.

Four 8½″ x 11″ cards have eight pictures glued on each of them, four along the left side and four along the right. All the cards have some of the same pictures and each card has some different ones. On 3″ x 3″ cards are statements that are true of one picture and sometimes of several pictures.

Pictures on the cards include: Baptism, preparation of Communion, ushering, choir practice, church school class, counting money, calling on a sick person, singing in congregational worship, and many others.

Some of the titles are: Jesus taught his disciples to do this. One way to praise God. Jesus began this practice at the Last Supper. Christians support the work of the church. Every member works for every other member. When we can't come to church, the church comes to us.

A spinner is used by each player in turn to direct him in what to do. The dial is divided into segments. Two of the segments are large and are marked TAKE ONE CARD. It is most probable that the spinner will point to one of those segments, and the game progresses. The smaller segments of the circle are marked TAKE TWO CARDS, GIVE UP ONE CARD, MISS ONE TURN, TAKE ANOTHER SPIN. If the arrow stops directly over a line, the player is allowed to spin again.

When a player is directed to take a card, he or she places it next to the picture he thinks it applies to, or returns it to the bottom of the pile of cards. If during the game a player gets a card that better describes a picture he has already titled, he may change the title beside the picture or sacrifice a title card in order to use the more accurate title. The player whose card is filled first is the winner. Each picture must be accompanied by a statement judged to be true by all players and a teacher if the players cannot agree.

STUMBLING BLOCKS AND STEPPING STONES

This board game has as its object the remainder of God's covenant with his people from earliest times to the present. It reviews the times of well-being and adversity.

The board is divided into small squares which begin in the center and wind round and round to the outside edges, ending in the lower right-hand corner with an arrow pointing to the future.

Events printed in green are positive and allow the player to advance his or her token forward. Events printed in red are negative and force the token backward, to stay where it is, or to begin all over again. One die thrown in turn directs the progress of the game. The person who reaches NOW first is the winner.

Positive events include: Creation, call of Abraham, birth of Isaac, David made king, birth of Jesus, the empty tomb.

Negative events include: Pharaoh makes Hebrews slaves, Hebrews worship golden calf, God's people in exile, Jesus is crucified, Stephen is killed.

FIRST AND SECOND GRADES

The tempo and the disposition of the teachers and learners in this room resemble an industrious kindergarten more than one of the other classrooms described. There are two reasons for this: (1) Reading is not required, though it can be used if a child is able, and (2) all the outcomes are the result of group, not of individual, effort.

There are differences too. The children are conscious that learning is taking place, partly because much of the content relates to Hebrew and Jewish life and customs, and partly because the teachers have about them an air of expectancy. In a kindergarten there might be a home living center with stove, table, chairs, and tea set. In this room for first- and second-graders, they ground grain, tasted goat's milk, and helped make unleavened bread. (In a discussion preceding a demonstration of a synagogue school, both boys and girls were open-mouthed in disbelief to hear that girls did not and indeed could not go to school and probably never learned to read. "I'd learn to read some way!" a girl exclaimed. "I'd ask my brother to teach me, and no one would know."

("If I was your brother, I'd learn you. That's awful," said the boy sitting next to her.)

Although the teachers were reluctant to experiment with informal drama, they found the children uninhibited and spontaneous, bringing their present-day values and life-styles to what they were learning of the past. Their affinity for dramatization may have been a characteristic of this particular group, but in a second year the interest has persisted. Perhaps the truly informal atmosphere of the room encouraged it. Most of us who work directly with children in drama have found that some don't like it, and some even hate it if they are singled out. But when drama is kept informal, most children like it. When with great enthusiasm we teachers exclaim: "That was wonderful!

Let's do it for . . ." it ceases to be informal. In this group, drama stayed informal. There was never a stage, and almost always everyone was involved.

Sometimes unfamiliarity with the subject and setting is a deterrent to spontaneous drama.

The aforementioned discussion of little girls' rights blazed into drama when the Temple was described. A teacher told a story about the day Jesus was old enough to go with his father and no longer sat with his sisters and his mother. No discussion. The classroom was already set up separate and unequal, as the Temple. A sister said: "It's not fair. Jesus gets to go in there, and we can't." But we can't keep the twentieth century from twentieth-century children. The boy playing Jesus was left alone with the learned men and said, "Hey, my sisters would really like to come in here." And one of the learned men said, "Okay, tell them to come next Sunday."

The basic curriculum resources for the denomination were used. Preparation took far less time than for the older groups. There was no contracting with individuals and there was no checking an individual's finished product. One would think that the teachers would be gratified. But at first they weren't. And thereby hangs a warning or two.

Most people beginning with a degree of openness are almost neurotic in their curiosity about what others are doing. After all, the doors are open and the walls are down traditionally. We don't realize for even a year or two that openness leads to the development of individual style. Even after we teach for many years, some of us seldom completely trust our judgment of what a given group of children can, should, or will do.

These teachers heard the teachers of the older age groups talking about "mastery of content," "individual achievement," and "behavioral objectives." They were not at all certain what these slogans meant, but they were dead sure that they didn't have any and maybe needed some. It took two years before they saw the uniqueness of what they did for the children *while* they had them, and to prepare them *for* the time they went to the next group. Their children continued to like learning. The teachers of the third- and fourth-graders told them so.

The warnings: Never look at a classroom of your age group or another for anything but good ideas you might want to use in addition to the ones working already.

Never conclude, without making a careful investigation, that another group of teachers are more experienced, more talented, have more money, time, room, and love for those they teach. Do not assume someone knows the first and last word on open education. No one remembers the first, and we haven't heard the last. We are not all beginners, but we are all on the road. Those of us who like it best have learned that we never get worse at what we're doing. We change. We try new ways with different people. But we spend little effort in the idle pastime of comparing ourselves to others.

A measure of the understanding that children have of this particular model of open education is evidenced by a comment of a younger brother to his older sister:

"What are you doing in here, Chucky? Go back to your room," his sister chided.

"Aw, come on! Let me see what you're learning."

FOREWARNING

This system which emphasizes observable outcomes and the consciousness of learning puts a heavy demand on the leadership. It requires discipline and hours of planning. Everyone learns shortcuts. The task becomes easier as you become familiar with the basic resources. When children catch on to the routines, learn to choose learning tasks, and find satisfaction in completing them, the burden of planning becomes lighter. It seems worthwhile.

Nonetheless, you can get tired. Rather than approach a unit or a season with dreary resolution, limit your content-centered units to high-energy times for both leaders and learners. Choose a less ambitious but equally enhancing style of learning and planning. The broadly graded models in the next chapter are useful for times when attendance is slim, when group achievement is set over individual learning, and when serendipity is a built-in asset. Back in the days before "serendipity" stepped out of the unabridged dictionary and appeared on coffeehouses, boutiques, and contemporary songbook covers, a Christian education professor called that built-in asset "room for the Spirit." She told her students that plans should be made carefully, so that when we vary from them for those welcome, unexpected reasons, we still have a road to follow to the point we intend to reach. That is open education.

3 Broadly Graded Church School

For years churches with schools of forty children or fewer have voiced displeasure with curriculum materials geared to classes of an average of ten or more of one age group. With counsel, a few would reluctantly experiment with broadly graded education. The complaints came in: Nonreaders can't keep up. Third-graders don't like to color and paste. Their attention spans vary too much at these ages. Fourth-graders are bossy. Fifth-graders are losing interest. Sixth-graders don't come.

After hearing about one more broadly graded educational disaster, an ancient hand at soothing harried spirits remarked: "What we'll have to do is make broad grading popular instead of necessary. Let's try it where we don't have to and see how it works." It was obvious to objective eyes and ears that those complaints were from places where *everybody* was expected to do *everything* at the same time. Of course third-graders are bored coloring or pasting what a first-grader can color or paste. And no wonder the sixth-graders won't come for that. But there was hope in the constant complaint about the bossy fourth-graders. Maybe they are the ones who are ready to start managing.

The first experiments were done in suburban churches with fewer children than they had once had but with enough to carry on in traditional age groups. Broad grading was a true alternative, not a last resort. One radical adaptation was accomplished in an open country church with twelve children in grades one through five. There were five under school age and only one, an eighth-grade boy, who was older.

The first principle that all of the experimenting churches worked on was to increase the quality and the variety of the education already provided, rather than to add new programs to it. As one of the lead teachers in First Church reported: "Children already came for an hour on Sunday morning. We decided to spend our energies improving that time before we asked for more!"

MODEL I

First Church is located in a suburb of fifteen thousand people. It is near recreational areas offering water sports in the summer and skiing in the winter. Attendance in grades two through five drops to twenty or twenty-five in the summertime and can climb to over fifty during the school year. Attendance, except for a small reliable core, is sporadic.

Before the change to a broadly graded program, children met in classes according to their grades in school. When a teacher was absent, two classes met together. One Sunday the superintendent told the third-graders to go into the second-graders' class and found herself on the scene of a small revolt. "We can teach ourselves," one third-grader told her.

"Would you rather go in with the fourth-graders?" she asked.

"No, we don't want to go in with anybody." They taught themselves that Sunday, or at least they thought they did.

The planners believed that this form of isolation need not be supported, but they did decide to bring the boys and girls into the planning. Second- through fifth-graders were given preference tests in their classes. They completed them with intense interest and a seriousness that goes with genuine responsibility. The current teachers made up the test based on one that had appeared in their educational resources.

Preference Test

This is a test to help you and your teachers decide which kinds of things you most want to do in church school. It is not a test to find out what you *know*. It is a test to show how you *feel* about the ways you learn. The only way to get 100 is to tell the truth. Put an "X" by any answer you think is true.

1. When I come to my class, I would like—
   - to help the teacher with supplies ______
   - to walk around and then find something to do ______
   - to read ______
   - to talk with the others ______
   - to sing into the tape recorder and listen to my voice ______
   - to help somebody who is already working ______

2. When I come to my class, I don't like—
   - to sit and be quiet ______
   - to sing ______

to work with people I don't know _______
to stand around and do nothing _______
to work by myself _______
to decide what to do _______

3. When we start a project, I like—
to finish it even if it takes the whole time _______
to do a little each Sunday _______
to have it be something to take home _______
to do one big thing and keep it at church _______

4. When we work with Bibles, I like—
to try to find the verses myself _______
to work with someone who reads better than I _______
to teach others how to find verses _______
to hear the story first and then find verses _______
to be recorder and write on the chalkboard _______

5. When we learn songs, I like—
to sing together from books _______
to sing along with a guitar _______
to study hard words and then learn the tune _______
to listen to a few songs and choose which one to learn _______
to learn the song at home and teach it here _______

6. When we have plays, I like—
to know exactly what to say and do _______
to make puppets _______
to direct the play _______
to be the main character _______
to make up my own words as I act _______

7. When we worship, I like—
to go to church with a friend _______
to learn about the service and then go _______
to pray and read the Bible in class _______
to know beforehand if I have to pray aloud _______

8. If we could go anywhere for church school, I would like—
   - to give a play at the old people's home ______
   - to visit another church ______
   - to go outside and take slides on location ______
   - to sing with our church choir ______
   - to go with my class to Communion ______
   - to take a party to a children's hospital ______

9. If we decided to be a club instead of a class, I would like—
   - to be president ______
   - to help plan things to do ______
   - to be a secretary and write to those who are absent ______
   - to make a bulletin board with club news ______
   - to invite others to be in our club ______

10. When we and the teachers plan together, I would like *them* to decide—
    - what to study ______
    - what projects to do ______
    - whether or not we can talk out loud ______
    - if we have to finish what we don't like to do ______
    - what to do with a person who is mean or won't work ______
    - how to make us behave ______
    - what work that we do gets put up ______

Adapted from *Teacher's Guide* (Revised), Grades 3–4/Year II.

The results of the inventory were not startling. The designated lead teacher reported that "the two who wanted to be president of the club also chose to be the main character in the play." The effect of having completed it, however, involved the boys and girls in the program as they never had been before.

The teachers also completed a preference test based on learning activities suggested in their previous materials. Then they compared them in an effort to spread their talents around and not restrict the boys and girls to one teacher's limitations. In the broadly graded grouping teachers worked in the area of their competencies. An outline of the first session of a unit will show how this was accomplished.

UNIT OBJECTIVE: To become familiar with the Biblical story of Creation from Gen., chs. 1 to 2:3.

SESSION OBJECTIVE: To become familiar with Gen. 1:1–8 and re-create that portion of the story in at least two ways.

Short-term work centers:
- Listening to tape recording of Gen. 1:1–8
- Listening to *The World God Made* at story circle
- Singing "Wherever I May Wander" (No. 36)
- Beginning practicing choral reading of Gen. 1:1–8

Group gathering:
- Retelling by children of Gen. 1:1–8
- Learning from music group "Wherever I May Wander"
- Explanation of various work centers and deciding who will work where
  (Tell them that when they hear the guitar they have five more minutes.)

Project centers:
- Beginning painted mural
- Starting "small world" box
- Making sun and moon with tissue paper glued to big window

Continuing choral reading
Beginning original script for filmstrip, *God's Wonderful World*

The unit on Creation began in July when the group was at its smallest. A surprisingly good range of ages attended throughout the summer, although the same pupils were not there each Sunday. The lead teacher was a leader with previous experience in the church school, but the other teachers were being oriented for work in the fall, should the experiment prove worth repeating.

Each week at the group gathering, the new approach was explained to newcomers, at first by the teachers and eventually by the hardy perennials who had come to be comfortable in the routine. With very little suggestion by the lead teacher the older children began working with and helping the younger ones by reading to them, helping them "put on a play," and explaining classroom rules. (This demonstration of concern was not as prevalent after the group increased in size by almost half.)

Probably because of the amount of movement, there were few problems with discipline stemming from restlessness. There were two rules, however, that sometimes caused displeasure: (1) What was started must be finished before going on to something else; and (2) the number of persons at each center was restricted by the type of activity, and that number was posted. When problems arose concerning these two rules, the children and adults gathered for "talk it over time" and came to a common understanding. The adults tended to be more lenient than the fourth- and fifth-graders, who looked upon the rules as sacrosanct. The teachers were not placed in a position of pitting their authority against any child's will. The authority was vested in the rules of the classroom, and decisions about violations were made cooperatively.

Toward the end of August a group evaluation period was planned near the close of a session. Questions were posted on a low easel and the children responded: What did you enjoy doing most during summer church school? What did you like least? What would you like to change? What would you like to do that we haven't done? What would you like to do more often than we did?

The discussion was lively and earnest. The younger children were able to answer the first two questions with conviction, but the older children were more adept at answering the more hypothetical ones. Both older and younger children cited trips out of doors as enjoyable and divided completely on the short interview with an astronomer. The older children would have repeated it; the younger children liked it the least.

One very quiet child when asked directly what he liked the most mumbled, "Watching what everyone does." He had one of the best attendance records, but seldom entered a group where he had to make an individual response. He listened to stories, sang with the group, and watched filmstrips.

A fourth-grade extroverted child said, "I like the acting and the no reading." Until this summer he had been a most disruptive child in the church school. The lead teacher reported that he was "bossy and loud but interested. An improvement," she added, "from the kid who traveled five miles on his chair each Sunday playing 'chicken' with his less reckless classmates."

The teachers and Christian education committee decided to continue the broadly graded program through November with the stipulation that if the group became too unwieldy as attendance increased, it would be divided into two broadly graded groups.

In October the group was divided, but the teachers continued to plan together. The two groups met together twice that fall—once for an All Saints' Day parade of banners and song, and once to hold an open house for the congregation.

During the month of December they celebrated Advent and Christmas in intergenerational workshops held before congregational worship. From January until Easter, the two groups flourished, and almost immediately after that, attendance was sporadic enough to merit only one group.

With all the changes, the morale of teachers and pupils stayed high, probably because the program belonged to all of them. The children clearly had a voice in their own learning and were encouraged and supported by adults around them.

MODEL II

Mt. Olive Church sat at an intersection of two county roads fifteen miles from a village. The school, a half mile down the village road, was no longer used for general education, and the children in the area went to a large community school by bus. Coming to Mt. Olive were eighteen children at the very most. Five were below school age. There were three first-graders, four second-graders, one fourth-grader, four fifth-graders, and one eighth-grader.

The youngest children met in an anteroom, and the elementary-age children met in two groups called primary and junior in the basement. The eighth-grader served as general assistant to the superintendent just to have something to do.

Attendance was good because it was expected of them. Adults came for church school classes, which met in the sanctuary, and the children came along.

The new minister was shared by another smaller church and arrived just in time to begin the service of worship each week without having seen the church school. The exceptions were in those months having five Sundays. On the fifth Sunday both congregations met at Mt. Olive for a union service at 10:45 after church school. On the first of these Sundays the minister visited the church school and found it a dreary environment indeed. Teachers read and children listened in the elementary grades. Teachers read and children colored in the preschool room. The eighth-grade boy took attendance, passed out take-home papers, and stood around a good bit.

Meeting with the official board, the minister voiced his concern about education in the church, especially of the children. The officers were neither surprised nor insulted. They agreed that the school had certainly had better days. "But there were more of us then, and not so many old ones" an officer said. "Why, some days there were sixty people here—children, young people, and adults. Now we have no young people but Harvey, and it's the grandparents bringing the youngsters."

The man was right. It was also true, however, that the schoolchildren didn't know one another well. They didn't even all ride the same school bus. The minister suggested that getting acquainted might be a first step in revitalizing the church and its school. Without realizing he was coining a phrase, he said, "Let's see that everyone here is an active member."

First Steps

With the minister's imagination as leaven, the superintendent and the woman who played the piano for worship met to consider possibilities for a brighter future for the church.

They looked together at the educational resources used by the children's classes. They had been selected about fifteen years before, the superintendent thought, when a previous minister's wife had been in charge of the church school. Though the present superintendent ordered the materials, she was not familiar with them.

The children below school age were using resources that assumed work at various interest centers about the room and a liberal amount of time in an activity period. The room where they met had only a table and chairs and the only activities were storytelling and coloring.

The school-age children used an interdenominationally produced series with teacher's quarterlies, pupil's workbooks, and teaching pictures. The teacher's quarterly suggested a variety of learning activities and the workbooks offered more. But in both the primary and junior classes, most of the activity was performed by the teachers.

The young minister was open in his criticism of the operation of the church school. "Our resources are fine for our purposes, but we aren't using them as they're intended."

"Well," the superintendent told him, "we're only volunteers."

"So is almost every church school teacher in the country. We can do better than this—anyone could," he replied.

"If you know where to begin," the superintendent said, "we'll do what you say."

"I want your ideas too," the minister told the two women.

The pianist laughed heartily. "You don't understand, Pastor. We don't have any ideas. Would things be so bad now if we'd had ideas?"

The superintendent mused: "No, we aren't a thinking people. We just carry on."

It was true for the time being. Those appointed to be leaders were not. The only leadership was that of the pastor. It was his job to do teacher education, reorganize the church school, and find signs of life in the congregation wherever he could.

Teacher Education

The teachers needed a new picture of education in the church. The minister contacted an educational consultant in a distant city, asking particularly where the teachers and leaders might observe a well-run church school with well-taught classes. He was sent the names of two churches, one in the county seat town and another in a suburb of a large city eighty miles away. He proposed that they visit both places. The official board agreed to send two representatives with the teachers, superintendent, and pianist.

The county seat church was across from the courthouse and drew enough children from the entire town to have an average attendance of about 150. Classes were in two-year groupings, and the administration was efficient. Most of what they saw would not be applicable to their situation with two remarkable exceptions: The children participated in a variety of activities in all age groups, and the very young children had a room equipped with a housekeeping center, dress-up clothes, a store, and a discovery corner.

"I could not have imagined how that interest center business looked," the superintendent said later. The lead teacher in the kindergarten gave the visitors a copy of a sheet for parents entitled "How We Get Work Done in the Kindergarten." It explained the purposes of the interest centers and related them to the ways young children learn.

The suburban church was a surprise. First- through fourth-graders were together in a large group. The church school coordinator explained: "We could have two groups of two grades each, but we like it this way. It all started when we had a child in fourth grade who couldn't read and was deeply embarrassed. We started a small broadly graded group, and the next year we put them all together."

The coordinator moved easily through the room without disturbing the activity at the various centers. Printed on the chalkboard was the list of centers, more for the teachers' benefit than for the children's.

The visitors were spellbound. In their report of the visit they said: "They had art, a puppet play, and a singing project going on all at the same time." "The children stood up more than they sat down, but there was no running around. They were all so busy and so contented."

The minister took notes at both churches in order to make references in the teacher education seminars. One anecdote he wrote down was crucial later on in the life of Mt. Olive Church, where their goal was "active" membership.

The large group of children had gathered to sit on the floor near the end of the hour. They were to see the puppet play, and it was all set up.

"Do you suppose we can go out and see if our crocuses are up?" a girl asked.

"Well," the teacher at the front of the group said, "we have seven minutes before church is to be out upstairs. The puppet play will just about fill that. What do you think we should do?"

"I want to give the play," one of the puppeteers said.

"It seems to me," one of the older boys opined, "that we could see the play and then look for the crocuses on our own time. We all know where they are."

No one disagreed and the show went on. This was genuine decision-making.

Another comment the minister had noted was: "There was no front to the room. It was a schoolroom for children, not for tables and chairs."

The pianist noted that there was no piano but more singing than she had ever heard at Mt. Olive.

No other experience, save their own first attempts, taught or encouraged the teachers and leaders more than the visit to the broadly graded classroom.

They attended the seminars the minister scheduled and, as the primary teacher said, "found out what a seminar is. It's talking and discussing with one another, not just listening to the minister talk." They learned how to read their educational resources and to plan centers. When each teacher reported, the others questioned and thereby learned. The morale was high before they began their own remodeling. What resulted was a scheme unlike anything they had seen.

The Scheme

The younger children used the anteroom with interest centers, no chairs and one small table. Art activities were done on the floor as they most often were at home. The story time found the teacher and the children on the floor.

The older children joined forces in the basement and used the entire room with less chaos than they had in separate groups.

On the fifth Sundays the children meet with the few boys and girls who come from the pastor's other parish. They are justly proud of their "new school," and from time to time invite the adults to visit them. The walls of the basement bear witness to what is being learned and experienced.

The adults are fully in approval of the evidence of new life, and the minister is hopeful of growing initiative by the teachers in the work of planning.

One of the few young fathers who comes on fifth Sundays from the other church saw his twin boys become active participants with children they didn't know well. "I stayed on the farm and ran it for Dad. Maybe the boys will too. But someday they'll belong to *this* church in pen and ink as well as in spirit. Our little church won't be. But I don't say that around the folks. We'll go on this way and one day close up. The church is what's inside the building, isn't it?"

Evaluation

The minister feels that he is still the only leader, but he is working toward the goal of seeing the teachers and leaders plan a quarter without his being present. "They work at their planning the way I learned do-it-yourself electrical installation," he reported, "one step at a time and slowly."

The teachers of the new group are not self-conscious in the church school. On the fifth Sunday following the beginning of the program, the minister was welcomed in the room. He believes that in this climate of openness the focus is on the children, and the teachers don't feel "on trial." Strangely enough, these same teachers, who a year before did nothing but talk to children, are concerned now with the quality of what children produce as evidence of what they know and learn.

It is very likely (to add an evaluation to an evaluation) that the minister's open-eyed, open-minded approach to solving educational problems is at the base of the teachers' feeling free to operate with or without him.

New Directions

The eighth-grade boy is now a high school sophomore, and everyone has moved up. There are no new members in the group and no losses except among the elderly in the church. That sole young person is a "born assistant." He spends about half of his time in each of the two children's groups, and attends the seminars. He is not an academic giant, but he works well with the children and the adults. Someone said to him on a fifth Sunday, "You ought to be a schoolteacher." And he answered: "Oh, no. Even if I worked hard all the time, I wouldn't be smart enough to teach school. But I'm smart enough to help."

The minister feels that this comment is one indication of the long-term low educational expectations of that rural community. Even as they improve their lot, they do not feel equipped even for the job they are doing well.

The minister is a goal setter. He has short-range and long-range goals. He would like to have a weekday school for elementary-age children of any faith. (There are many Roman Catholics in the community with no religious education.) He would like to see Mt. Olive become an observable model for small church educational enterprises for a large area. But his sustaining short- and long-range goal is to develop leadership in the church. "When I leave, the life of the church cannot go with me," he writes. "If they were impoverished when I came, they must not be when I leave."

They still are not a "thinking people," as the superintendent put it. They are accommodating. But the children are making real decisions weekly. They are leaders in a way their grandparents are not. And they will become leaders, some of whom will remain in the church.

The pianist is an institution in the church. Every child knows her and no child questions her presence whether or not music is involved.

The week before a fifth Sunday all the children were together to learn an "Alleluia" refrain to a hymn that the combined congregation would sing. The pianist said, "We'll let the adults sing it first, and then we'll sing it."

"Phooey," said a third-grader. "Why don't we sing it first and show them how?" And so they did. In a day when extroverted urban children are numbing their parents, there are still young people and children who lead only by default of their leaders and by no desire of their own.

MODEL III

Although there is much to learn from this model, it is included for what it neglected to do. It was billed as "Discovery Time" and might well have been called "Dabbling Hour."

Several adult leaders, the minister, and his wife felt that the church school of a small suburban congregation was not lively or colorful enough for their present crop of children. They were also having a difficult time convincing persons to teach for an entire school year, with vacations and ski weekends.

Their solution was to utilize the church hour in an open classroom for grades one through six. What they did ultimately cannot be called "education." If anything, it was exposure to adults in the church taking their turns at Discovery Time. Some of them read stories, others shared their hobbies, and a few of them showed slides of trips they had taken. Occasionally, a movie was shown. Seasonal holidays were celebrated and adult guests were asked to speak to the children.

The open concept continued somehow, and the children, though not enthusiastic, were not bored. One day a young couple leading the group brought bread dough out of which the boys and girls made small beads which they strung on wire and embellished with a tassel of yarn for a necklace. After a thoroughly enjoyable time of baking their necklaces and shellacking them, the man told a story of the significance of their jewelry.

In the afternoon following Discovery Time one of the third-graders had an adult guest in his home.

"I want to give you something, Mrs. Sterling. We made it in Discovery Time."

"Why, thank you, Andy. It's done very well. What did you find out about it?" she asked.

"It's Indian or something. But it's made of bread dough and baked and shellacked and all that. This-here yarn means something. But I'm not sure what. Maybe it's not Indian. Maybe it's Arabic. Or African. Maybe my sister knows."

His sixth-grade sister said that she had helped the woman leader clean up and had not heard the story. "That's what's frustrating to me," she announced. "You wonder about something all week and there's nobody there the next time who can give an answer."

The program goes on as aimless as ever and probably will until the congregation's bag of tricks is empty. The experience in itself seems to be more positive than negative. What is missing in the corporate life of the church is an educational endeavor. They could go in one of two directions: transform their open classroom to open education or hold an educational event at some other time. The program as it is would profit by better planning, so that even as a misnamed discovery period it could have more substance and direction.

One cannot help noticing and commending the give-and-take intergenerationally at church-wide events. The boys and girls have become acquainted with many adults other than conventional church school teachers. The kind of sharing that they do has a place in the church, but it should not be confused with education or substituted for it. Even open education is a deliberately planned, purposeful activity.

Much of what Discovery Time was seeking, and to some extent accomplishing, might be done more effectively as a series of planned intergenerational events for the whole church to enjoy. In such events the goal is fellowship with and appreciation of other people. The occasions are not intended to teach facts of the faith or to build on previous learnings. What we do in the church involving children should be memorable and worthy of memory. Surely, planned learning experiences should not be excluded from one's backward look at childhood in the church.

4 Planned Intergenerational Events

An earnest, fairly unimaginative veteran of many week-long leadership schools was struggling with intergenerational education. "We're right back where we started. The old Sunday school had everybody all together for singing and Bible-reading, and discussions. Are we supposed to *like* that again?"

"I don't know about you," her instructor replied, "but I never did like it, and I won't start now."

Nobody knows for sure when the church's emphasis shifted from family nights to intergenerational events. But it was the institution's critics who pushed the church in that direction. "There is a family night series at Plymouth Church during January," a professor of sociology told his class. "That means that the family gets into a car, goes to church, and each member goes to a different room."

The minister of a city church wrote of "the offense to the aged, the single, and the one-parent families" when church education literature assumed the nuclear family to be a preferred status.

As the criticism rolled in, the old forms had fairly well lost their luster, and many churches discarded them for more workable options. That is when intergenerational education became the untested panacea for ailing church life.

At their best, intergenerational events did improve the quality of church life, because the church family emerged as a living organism. At their worst, they were meaningless copies of what worked elsewhere, and all that can be said in their favor is that they didn't do much harm.

Two principles were at work in those churches where their attempts were successful. *They had a reason for making the events intergenerational and they did not expect the events to do the whole educational job.* Of the ten projects included here, only three were adaptations of programs from other churches, and they were seasonal projects. The others grew out of seeds within the congregations. There is no reason to think that they couldn't be tailored to another church's needs, but here they represent evidence that appropriate programs for the entire church family are welcomed and add a needed dimension to the shared life.

PROJECT I. ADVENT WORSHIP WORKSHOP

In a suburban church with an increasing number of retired persons and a decreasing but still substantial number of children and youth, corporate worship had not changed for years. In a unit about worship third- and fourth-graders were to study the order of service, become familiar with the hymnal, learn congregational responses, and "endure a sermon," as the minister phrased the last learning task. As an outgrowth of the unit the boys and girls visited three other churches in their neighborhood. At the Roman Catholic service they experienced a contemporary mass alive with guitars, a folk-singing group, banners with symbols, and worship in the round.

"Why can't we have fun at church like that?" a fourth-grade boy asked one of the teachers.

"Maybe we can sometime," he was told. The teacher reported the experience and the remark to their pastor.

"It would be hard to change the older folks, I'm sure," he said. "They like to know what's going to happen."

The teacher dropped the matter until a fall planning meeting was held to decide on seasonal emphasis in the church school. The teachers and educational committee members decided to interrupt sequenced study during Advent and do a workshop each week as the Lutheran churches in the area did. They assigned a committee of three—the third- and fourth-graders' teacher was one of them—to work on details. From members of the Lutheran churches, they discovered that the Advent workshops varied from one family night when Advent wreaths were made for home use to an intergenerational series of workshops culminating in a Christmas Eve service.

They found their launching pad right there. The committee planned four workshops an hour in length. Each workshop was held in the church dining room with a symbol and banner center, a choral speaking group, a litany and prayer writers' center, and a decorations center. The leader at each center just happened to be a retired person. The committee looked for expertise, and that is where they found it. Young children and older ones who did not care to read and write chose the decorations center and the symbol and banner center. The choral speaking group was large and grew larger. The women who led it suggested that on the last of the four weeks, they become a singing choir instead, and have a carol sing.

Individuals were not expected to comply to stated objectives, and no one had to pursue work at a center he or she disliked. The projects at each center, however, had to result in something that could be used by the group planning the Christmas Eve service.

The workshop was well received. Men and women who had long since given up church education both as teachers and as learners entered enthusiastically into the activities. Young people taught and learned from their elders. Some of the elementary-age children attached themselves to elderly people, older than their grandparents. The young middle-aged people were the least likely to mix or be sought after. (In an evaluation meeting, a man of that age said: "That's no surprise to me. We're the parents, the schoolteachers, and the cops of their world. Who wants us?")

The Christmas Eve service was truly a celebration of worship and song. The newly made banners were hung between windows in the sanctuary. The worship committee had worked hard to incorporate the original litany and prayers with the Scripture selections of the choral speaking groups. A short section of W. H. Auden's "For the Time Being, A Christmas Oratorio," performed by the same group, took the place of a sermon. The children had particularly enjoyed antiphonal singing the Sunday before and learned "While by My Sheep" and "Lo, How a Rose E'er Blooming" with adults and youth singing opposite them. (In a written evaluation a senior citizen answered "What have you learned that you did not know before?" with "When I listened to the children singing I learned I couldn't cry and sing at the same time.")

The decorations were all over the church. There was a Jesse tree in the sanctuary, a tradition borrowed from the Lutheran churches in the area. It was decorated with symbols from the Old and New Testaments related to the lineage of Jesus and Jesus himself. The very young children had helped make wreaths out of tissue paper strung on coat hangers. Older elementary children made boxwood trees which were intended as Christmas Day gifts to hospital patients. And on the afternoon of Christmas Eve two women and a man worked with two high school boys on a Della Robbia fresh fruit wreath, a yard in diameter, to go after the service to a church-supported lodging for transient men in the nearby city.

It may be true that, as one of the choral speaking group said, "Anything would have worked that night." It is also true that no one in the congregation was a bystander or a spectator. The work of the participants was the substance of the service of worship. What started as a vague wish to have fun at church was the beginning of a new congregational life-style.

The Sunday after Christmas was a letdown. The fifth- and sixth-graders were few in number and restless. "We don't like being alone," a girl told one of the teachers.

"You're not alone, Julie. We're all here." Her teacher chuckled.

"Mr. Hampton and Miss Taylor and Mrs. What's Her Name with the allergy to glue. Where are they?" the child pursued.

At worship. That is where they were. And it wasn't quite what it had been to them just before Christmas.

Needless to say, the Advent Worship Workshop is a repeatable, intergenerational event.

PROJECT II. LENTEN POD PROJECTS

In the previous project, service was woven into the fabric of the event. In this project service is the goal. It took place in an affluent church in a downtown neighborhood of a large city. One of the ministers had an overpowering urge to teach well-to-do people to give more than money. "Money," he told them, "is the easiest thing for you to give. Give of yourselves." They agreed about the money but not about themselves.

During Lent there had been a tradition of taking an

offering for interdenominational help in emergencies such as earthquakes, floods, and famines. These people did well at "giving in the dark." It was an income-tax deduction. What would they do with donating themselves?

All who chose to participate signed up to become part of a pod. Each pod was instructed to find a way or ways to earn money for the Lenten offering. If two or more pods wanted to work together, they could. A whole family could join a pod or the members could join separate ones.

The ways to earn money were approved or improved by a committee of the official board of the church to avoid duplication and to assure that the pod projects were worthy services for which the community would be willing to pay.

Pod projects were varied: washing cars at a shopping center service station; making and selling dried-apple dolls, novelty candles, flowers in plastic cubes, and macrame flower pot holders; quilting; holding a community garage sale, a Maxwell Street odds and ends bargain day, and a sale of nearly new outgrown young children's clothes.

The local weekly paper sent someone to take pictures of the Maxwell Street bargain day and ended up with a full-page feature of the pods at work. There were groups shown at work in kitchens, in garages, on street corners, and in the church parlor. In each at least three generations were visible, and at the car wash four.

In evaluating the whole project, the committee of the official board felt that the interaction between church family members was the most worthwhile aspect. Least desirable was the lack of information that pod groups had about the reason for the fund-raising. The chairman said that any Salvation Army Santa Claus knew more about his cause than most of the participants. One young mother reported that her twin girls were selling dried-apple dolls in the neighborhood for the "Merchendeze." When a parent on the street called her, she explained about the emergency fund to the delight of the caller.

In another year the group decided to make the event more educational at the outset through available filmstrips and printed materials and to match the money earned with money from the church members themselves. The project, adapted from one described in a denominational periodical, was hastily launched, but the committee learned by doing and intends more careful planning for a second year.

PROJECT III. PENTECOST PICNIC

In a wave of nostalgia a member of the oldest adult Bible class pleaded for an "old-fashioned Sunday school picnic for the kids." The minister, superintendent, and a teacher were less than enthusiastic.

"Why for the kids, Elton? You're part of the Sunday school too," the minister cajoled him. "You'd probably win the three-legged race with Teddy Harmon if he's learned to walk yet."

The superintendent brightened. "Now that kind of a picnic I'd go for. Less eating and more entertainment. Maybe we could do something as a whole church. St. Norbert's has a blowout every year at Pentecost."

That was the spark that ignited the fire of Pentecost at Clinton Avenue Church. It wasn't a picnic, it was a holiday. On Pentecost Sunday three things were carefully planned: (1) a highly participatory contemporary service of worship, (2) a balloon trip, and (3) a picnic in a city park.

The Service of Worship

Children are accustomed to attending corporate worship at Clinton Avenue Church, and older people are accustomed to them as well. Not too much is done to accommodate them aside from the freedom they have to move around. For this service the kindergarten through sixth grade learned the first stanza of "Now Thank We All Our God" in order to sing it with the congregation.

The children were familiar with the folklike songs sung to guitar accompaniment, and they knew how to respond in a litany of praise. What they weren't expecting was the Pentecost play in place of the sermon. Senior high young people with the help of three young men from the church's congregation wrote and produced a simple drama showing the downcast, waiting disciples, the same people touched by the Holy Spirit, and the congregation responding to Peter's sermon. The play ended with the reception and recognition of new members by the pastor.

The Balloon Trip

At the time of the offering, everyone was given a helium-filled balloon on a string with a card for the person's name attached. The card said, "Rejoice! Jesus is King." The congregation recessed to the lawn and sent the balloons aloft. Some of the recorded comments reflected the spirit of the day. "Nobody's ever too old for a gas balloon," an elderly lady chuckled. "Good-by, balloon. Go find a kid in Kentucky who wants you," an elementary-age child shouted. "It's like Fourth of July," a young girl commented, "only prettier." "Mine broke!" a child shouted. "That's okay. Somebody will find it sooner, that's all," he was told.

The Picnic

Eating was incidental. The major interest and curiosity were the games and competitions. Any age could qualify and any number could play. Prizes were more balloons of gargantuan proportions distributed by an elderly lady in a wheelchair who looked like a character out of a folktale holding a colorful bouquet of six-foot-long balloons. Both participants and spectators had a good time. And old Elton commented when the minister thanked him for having the idea, "Sunday school picnics aren't what they used to be; they're better."

The evaluation by the committee was largely positive. By the time the evaluation session was held two of the balloon cards had been sent back to the church, one local and another from a far suburb. One balloon had been caught in a tree and the far-flung one had eventually broken. The official board voted to repeat the event in its entirety but decided to look into a country area for the picnic, simply because people would enjoy getting out of the city. "We're no Chicago in size and complexity," a woman commented, "but we're in a big city in a big country. So let's see some of it." They know they face difficulty in finding another service of worship as appropriate. It will also be difficult to repeat the play. Surprise was an element in its success, and that would not be so another year. What they have in their favor is a tradition, though only two years old, of children's presence in corporate worship and an accepting group of older adults.

The first three projects described here were seasonal and in one form or another repeatable. A minister of education read over the descriptions of the Lenten Pod Projects. He said: "Poor, dumb Christians. Will we ever learn? *Easter* is the high point of the Christian year. If that isn't the culmination of Lent, forget Lent and Christian service. Join the Rotarians, and do good to others."

He was asked, "What would you have done differently?" And he knew, 1-2-3-4-5-6.

1. Teach those people that the second mile never ends; it's always the extra, past what we've done in the interests of others. Those people's burden is having more than they need and not knowing what it's like to live on the well-meaning, sporadic generosity of folk like themselves.

2. Make the project Biblical from the beginning. Proclaim the gospel from the start. And not, "It is more blessed to give than to receive." No! "Love your enemies, do good to those who hate you." And no matter what a businessman says, don't let your right hand know what your left hand has to give.

3. Focus the project on Easter. Let everybody in on the story: Jesus is with us as Christ.

4. Make the money changing an incidental, light affair. You're making and selling in order to know one another, not to make money. You've got that already; you want more, that's all. Get it from wherever you can; those flood and earthquake victims need it. But be ready to defend your cause and know as much as you can about it. Do you know what selling a pig in a poke is? That's what it is: asking for money you will spend any way you want. Don't dump that on people who are willing to give. They are worth more than that. They are worth teaching why people need their money.

5. Be honest about money. Sometimes old clothes don't do. They don't buy eggs in most markets. You need bills and coins. Money buys blankets, soap, and yes, old clothes in their time. People who have a lot of it should give a lot of it, because a lot of people don't have much in this country and elsewhere.

6. Easter is the Christian's Independence Day. Let our children celebrate with us before they grasp historical sequence. Let them know its importance before they learn its significance. Our service during Lent is our Thanksgiving for what happened at Easter. Celebrate Easter with horns, voices, colors, proclamation, and the smell of lilies if you like, but include the noise and awe of children for their edification as well as for ours.

About the other two projects for Advent and Pentecost he had no suggestions. "About Easter," he admitted, "I'm sensitive. I may never decide when to celebrate our church's birthday—at Easter or Pentecost. But at Easter where I am we celebrate Abundant Life."

At the church where he has worked for fifteen years only persons over thirty remember dull Easter services of worship and they don't want to return to them.

PROJECT IV. CELEBRATE AGE

At a city neighborhood church a core of adults of increasing age were charter members. Younger parents and their children came and went from apartment buildings to newly bought houses farther out. The leadership was almost completely made up of the aging charter members, who had deep loyalty to the survival of the church. They wanted to attract and to know the younger adults and their children, but they were short on ideas. They had just completed a search for a pastor when this project was planned. It was appropriate that they had been looking for "a younger man," and chose someone sixty-two years old.

The originator of "Celebrate Age" is a retired teacher and administrator who specialized in curriculum design. Her objective was for the church community to "acknowledge through enjoyment the age of a person, whatever it is." She planned for one hour following the ten o'clock service of worship for the first Sunday of September preceding Labor Day. ("*The New York Times* doesn't get to the ragged edge of the East until noon today," she pronounced in explanation of the hour.)

Her "committee" met once and was made up of representatives from the church school, youth, young parents, and the official board. The honorary member was a four-year-old girl who came with her mother and provided the name if not the idea for the activity center for young children. Three times in ten minutes as the adults examined craft items, pictures, and collections she wailed, "I can't *see!*"

Every center was a place to do what "you are old enough to do, taught by someone old enough to know how to do it well." The centers were set up in a vast area used for the sanctuary in the church's heyday, and abandoned as a new addition was built. One rather large corner area was walled off with low supply shelves for toddlers and a few babies. Everyone was there celebrating age doing what they could do because they were *old* enough. No one ever said "young enough."

Here are the centers as they were set up:

"I Can't See!"

At this center there were long, low adjustable classroom tables. Children could sit or stand. Adults generally stood. The signs for readers said, "Please handle," "Smell and guess," and "Try me." There were conch shells to hold to one's ear; *real* clay from the outdoors to mold and have baked later; detergent, water, and an eggbeater for foam making; and the makings of a coal garden among other things. The man in command is a retired policeman turned potter who serves as a school guard. Many children knew him and flocked about him as if he were a department store Santa Claus. He barked orders and maintained a well-run, industrious center. A three-year-old boy was listening to the conch, put it down, and said to the leader, "What was that stuff they was smellin'?"

"Oh, you're not old enough to do that," the man of the law said.

"I am three," he declared and held up three fingers.

"Okay. Smell and guess," the old man said.

"Tabasco sauce," was the answer. It was.

Teach and Learn

At this center were a weaver, a braider, a marzipan maker, a whittler, a leather tooler, an autoharpist, and a woman who transcribed braille with both a stylus and a braillewriter. The directions specified that these instructors would teach one person at a time giving an opportunity to work with the material or equipment.

What happened was unfortunate but understandable. A crowd of spectators gathered in front of each instructor until there was no room to work and no way of knowing who was next in line as a learner. With the exception of the whittler, the artisans went elsewhere in the church with a few followers. That move alleviated the congestion, but it deprived many at the "Fair" from seeing expertise in action. It was probably folly to assume that so many instructors could constitute one center rather than seven.

Collectors Corner

This center was plain fun for every collector seven years old and beyond. The participants brought and shared coins, butterflies, photographs, stamps, and recipes. There were three generations of teachers and learners. A woman in charge of the center was asked what she collected. She said, "People," and then added, "in groups." She is a retired social worker. She reported hearing a young boy say to a distinguished elder statesman of the church, "Now you wouldn't say that if you really *knew* butterflies."

Tasting Bee

This center was the hit, because the young parents outdistanced the old ones with ethnic dishes. Persons who had appreciated amalgamated Middle American or Ragged American East cuisine became fans of Italian, Greek, and

Slovak cooking. The young parents taught the old, and the young men were the gourmet heroes. One Italian girl of eight with her mother was showing how to roll out homemade pasta without a machine. They had commercial and homemade pasta to taste to prove the worth of their efforts. Most of the participants brought the food with the recipe. The Greek *filo*, tissue-thin pastry used in the spinach pie recipe, was a curiosity. "Do you make that at home like she makes her pasta?" a young man was asked. "No, no. I buy it at the bakery. Everybody does. Once they must have made it at home, but you know what happened. One was better than all the rest, and he became the *filo* king and opened the bakery."

The woman in charge of Tasting Bee entries is the acknowledged church supper queen. The more people and recipes she added to her list, the more elated she became. "No chicken pie," she told the chairman on the phone, "no 'add mushroom soup and bake.' Those kids are doing things I never heard of. I can't wait!" Those "kids," some of them, were forty to forty-five. Celebrate age!

This church will repeat the event at the same time next year. Members have become friends because of that interaction of interests. And new members will participate in place of those who leave. The obvious strength in the organization comes from one woman, but in time she may teach others the essentials of good programming. The chairman was asked, "What of this roaring success was most beneficial to the church?"

"Conversation!" she exclaimed. "You should hear the noise after services. We used to have a 'friendship time' just after announcements and just before offering. We'd smile and shake hands behind, beside, and before. Then we had 'Celebrate Age.' Our new minister won't have it. It was too hard to stop. He's right. I heard a voice over all others one

Sunday, 'I tried your *osso buco,* and it's smashing!' That can wait."

The planning the woman engineered was skillfully done. Chairmen of centers were named and where crafts, collections, and recipes were needed, entrants were to call the person in charge. At the same time, committee members called persons they knew to have interests and skills to share. It might have been as appropriately named, "Celebrate Size." In a large, urban, downtown church, it might never have had the impact it had in a medium-sized church in a once-established neighborhood. And without a former teacher at the helm, children might not have been encouraged to enter. She spoke directly to children to invite them to contribute collections and recipes.

The new minister called on this guiding light in his first weeks in the parish. He expressed hope of continued "interrelationships of generations."

"You're an agreeable fellow," she told him, "and I hope you do well; we need you. But ditch that language. Jesus said, '*Love* one another,' and I don't know how you can do it without *knowing* one another. That's what we aimed at. And that's what we hit."

In talking of people not related to the church but to the school system she said: "I wish they wouldn't borrow our language. We need theirs."

PROJECT V. NOBODY KNOWS

This is a money-raising project that has been used in several places with success where publicity has preceded it with imagination.

The purpose is to raise money quickly for an acute need the givers are not aware of, and where there is a reason to keep the secret.

In one church a gradual state of unemployment of

well-paid executives resulted in unpaid college fees and impending loss of property. The need was common knowledge, but because no one knew the precise recipient, the self-respect of those not accustomed to receiving was intact. As one of the planners commented, "It could be any one of us any day."

Everything people bring to sell has an exact price. It is not an auction. Publicity for the event can be assigned to one group or performed by the various age groups represented on the committee. In one church the young people made posters as reminders: a depicted Snoopy with Charlie Brown putting a price on the doghouse; a man looking at his bulging garage workroom and saying: "How can I ever find a thing I want? Nobody Knows." And on the day of the sale one young man strode back and forth in front of the church in a sandwich board that read, "I gave the shirt off my back to Nobody Knows."

Those involved seem to agree that part of the enjoyment is the secrecy. The planning committee should not know for whom or for what the proceeds of the sale are intended. Their skills should be those centered about being able to publicize and organize the event within two weeks' notice, so that the need is alleviated quickly and the enthusiasm for doing it is still high. The main purpose of the event is service to one another; enjoying the performing of a service is the bonus.

PROJECT VI. TRIP OF A LIFETIME

This was a simply executed project begun by a small group of couples in the church. From sheer interest it became an intergenerational event.

On a warm, sunny day the church sponsored a trip to the shore for chronically ill, permanently hospitalized persons. Living ninety miles away, some of the hospitalized adults had never seen the ocean. Upon inquiring initially at the hospital, the committee chairman found the administration most appreciative of the offer, especially for those persons who had little family contact by way of visits or occasional short trips home.

An orderly and a matron supervised getting the patients in and out of the cars and wheelchairs, enjoying a day at the shore themselves. They were a necessary part of the event in that they helped persons converse with one another. Some of the hospitalized persons were so short on experience, they were awed into silence or shyness. The presence of young children delighted some of the guests as they watched them playing on the beach.

"It's a trip of a lifetime for me," a young woman told the driver as she was taken from the car at the end of the day.

"For me too," he said; and he turned to his wife with, "and I'm a crusty M.D."

PROJECT VII. HIKING FOR CLIFF DWELLERS

An eighty-one-year-old outdoorsman came to live with his daughter's family in a city apartment. He was an expert hiker and a former teacher. At the church one Sunday he asked a group of young people if they liked to hike. They told him about Scout hikes and he told them about hiking the Appalachian Trail. He had been over the entire trail and some places many times. He would like, he said, to take some folks over one of the easier portions of the trail.

He made three trips during the summer: one with Scouts, another with families, and the last with any persons ten years old and above who had never hiked before. The inexperienced practiced before they went and were taken on one of the easier portions of the trail.

At one point, while the family group was resting, a

free-lance photographer and future writer stopped to inquire about the group. The prized leader was sound asleep about fifty feet away.

"You have to stop a lot for the old fellow, I guess," he commented.

"No, sir. He has to stop for us," one of the children told him. "He's been hiking for sixty-five years. We just started."

Apparently there was little going on in the world, the region, or the town, because pictures of the group and the awakened leader appeared on the first page of the daily newspaper.

The church has taken great pride in the efforts of this elderly man with the members. He is a popular presence at the coffee hour, not so much as a curiosity anymore, but as a helpful friend.

The following three intergenerational events are family-centered. They arose out of needs that family members expressed in relationship to their involvement in the church. They are not described in great detail, because the plans were particular solutions to specific problems. The manner in which they were solved is more important to other families than the details of the solutions.

PROJECT VIII. GETTING READY FOR THE LORD'S SUPPER

In churches where children are admitted to the Lord's Table with the parents' permission, agreement among families or between members of official boards is uncommon.

In one church, concerned parents organized a study group of four sessions led by the minister and involving the children from time to time in activities that would help them learn about the Sacrament. The adults read the words used in the administration of the Sacrament, discussed ways of varying the service to make it more visual to children, and learned a great deal about the centrality of the service to the life of the worshiping community. As one woman said, "I'm wondering about things I never thought of before."

The children examined Communion ware, made bread that was used in the service of corporate worship after the study group was over, and were told stories from the Bible about the Last Supper and subsequent reenactments in the early church. Older children participated in Bible study and became acquainted with the words of the institution of the Lord's Supper.

The minister expected more controversy than came out of the group of adults. What happened was that the parents were so ill informed and uninformed that by the time they examined facts and pondered concepts, they were not in a mood for controversy. They wanted to learn and experience more. Conversations at home with the children only heightened their desire for exposure to what had now become a mystery.

The order of service at the next Lord's Supper was changed very little from what had gone before. The worshipers were told of the source of the bread and the study of some of the families. The children had learned to sing the first stanzas of the hymns. During the distribution of the elements a young child whispered to her sister, "Are you gonna take it?" The older girl ignored her question. "Donna, I want to know are you . . . ?"

The minister looked at them and smiled broadly. "When you eat the bread and drink the wine, remember Jesus."

"I'll take some," the young child said aloud.

PROJECT IX. SUBSTITUTE GRANDPARENTS

In a new housing development outside a large city, the families suffered from an isolation most of them had not known before. The church that some of them attended had members of long standing and some more families similar to them from other developments. But no one was particularly friendly.

"Always before when we moved, we fit into the neighborhood and into the church. What's wrong here?" a woman asked the pastor on one of his home visits.

"You think there's something wrong with the place?" he asked.

"Well, I'm no different. Bill hasn't changed." She shrugged.

"Do other people complain to you?" her husband asked.

"Yes. They complain. And they change."

"They change?" the woman asked. "How do they change?"

"They seem to become unfriendly," the minister said directly.

The minister told this vignette in a sermon one Sunday, and said, "Any of you who would like to change the ending of my story, join me after church in the narthex."

Twenty-five people met with him for a defensive, spirited session. The minister summarized at one point: "Okay, we know what we don't like. What do we want instead?"

It developed that many of the residents of the developments got up very early to commute to work, got home late, and went to bed early. That ruled out the old church supper and evening meetings.

"My kids miss having grandparents," one man said, "and I miss having older people around. Every adult in the development is the same age."

"We never thought you wanted us at all," a dignified, striking, white-haired woman said icily.

What emerged was a retreat for young families with older people gathered for peacemaking and understanding rather than what some might call fellowship. The children got to know one another rather quickly. The adults resorted to formal get-acquainted procedures at the beginning, and gradually found some common ground and became more relaxed. The young children and the older people were akin by the time lunch was over and one child actually took his nap on his "grandmother's" lap.

After a day and a half of discussion and play the adults voted to spend some Saturdays at play just to get to know one another. "I hate to be near so many people without knowing any of them," a young woman exclaimed.

And an old resident summed up the feelings of many of them, "We get depressed seeing one development fill up after another, without ever feeling you're part of the township."

Both the young families and the grandparents have to remind themselves to take time to be thoughtful. But they are improving.

PROJECT X. FAMILY WORSHIP

"I have never been to a family service of worship I felt was for my family," a young man said at an official board meeting. A request had come to the board once more to gear the short, early service to families with young children. The minister was willing to try.

What evolved as a satisfactory solution took the better part of a year. When it began, the people who asked for it came with their children. A story was told in place of a sermon, and the music was largely of the folk variety. It was not what they were used to, and it was not what they wanted. The minister asked for the cooperation of the church school teachers, and together they worked out plans for congregational participation through experimental units of worship and study in the classrooms.

Sunday by Sunday the times together became more significant. Children and youth read Scripture. Sometimes guitars were used to accompany singing, but with great hymns of the church, the organ was played. Stories were still told, but occasionally the group had conversations and discussion instead. One Sunday the minister asked for prayers of concern after a congregational conversation. Adults and children responded alike. "After that," the pastor commented, "everything we did worked. We were a worshiping, caring community."

The service is always informal. It is never attended by more than forty persons, mostly families, but the singing has vitality and variety. Often young children are given tambourines, castanets, and bells to accompany the singing. Filmstrips and slides are shown now and then. But it is the quality of the response of the total congregation to the worship of God and to the needs of one another that sets these services apart from their former self-conscious attempts to be different. Worship is not imposed upon the gathered community. It is an expression from them.

The minister was asked to lead a workshop at a summer leadership school for people interested in "alternate forms of worship." He replied: "I know so little about this subject I could not possibly teach others what to do or even give them ideas to work on themselves. We don't have a bundle of material resources here. We have a group of people who want to come together to hear the Word and respond to it. Very little that I did made this community come to be. We met and God was in our midst."

These ten projects in which generations interact tell us two things: Persons of diverse ages can be enriched by coming together in the church for specific reasons, and no single pattern of any of these projects can be satisfactorily transplanted without pruning and tending in its new environment. In the next chapter where individuals with special needs are considered as active participants in the new openness in the church, it is even more evident that involved persons shape viable programs that become unique creations. The life of such programs depends on the people they serve.

5 Inclusive Classrooms

TO INCLUDE OR NOT TO INCLUDE

"We'd like to come to your church," a woman said to her new neighbor, "but our Barbara doesn't fit into church school, and one of us has to be home with her."

"What is her difficulty?" the neighbor asked, assuming, she said later, that Barbara was severely retarded.

"She's in a wheelchair, a victim of cerebral palsy. She goes to the elementary school at the Center, but they're prepared for her there," the girl's mother replied.

"I don't see why she couldn't come to our church school. There are two steps from the parking lot to the ground level where the children's classroom is. And we can use a ramp."

"There's only one classroom?"

"It's an open classroom for first through fifth grades. The children love it. So do the leaders," her neighbor explained. "I help out now and then. Bring your daughter to visit next Sunday. I'll come with you. If it's a good experience, she'll want to come back."

In a well-operated open classroom where children are productive learners, there is room for a person like Barbara.

There is room for a deaf child or a blind one. Teachers have learned in such a classroom how to help children participate in their own learning and contribute to the life and learning of the whole group. Giving plans some thought and effort, the teacher can incorporate activities for a child with a physical impairment or learning difficulty.

Although a broadly graded situation is most adaptable to a program for a child with a sensory handicap, any open classroom can accommodate itself with the help of a buddy system. The ratio of teachers to children who need special help is one to one. That means that when the designated buddy is to be absent, a substitute must be there.

One-to-oners have been engaged in work with mentally retarded persons in the church for a long time. But the church has not served the fewer persons with other learning disabilities and handicaps as well. An individual church is not likely to have a great many blind, deaf, or cerebral-palsied children within a generation. They are not likely, either, to know what to do with one except to give the parents materials to work with at home. With one person in charge of her welfare, Barbara could manage to get to the classroom, to participate in independent learning activities, and to contribute to the group's learning.

The rule, if there can be one for all children who need constant supervision, is that if the experience is constructive for the special child and not detrimental to the other children and teachers, it is well worth the time and effort to include the child. There are certain emotionally disturbed and hyperkinetic boys and girls who cannot accommodate to a weekly church school group and should not have to. There are some children with multiple handicaps who receive little benefit from the group experience and whose constant care and disruption tax both teachers and children beyond their ability to cope. The decision to include or not to include is always an individual one, and it should always be rooted in the good that can come from it to all of those involved.

ONE-TO-ONERS

The buddy system for disabled children operates from the time they are brought to their buddies until the time they are called for to go home. The educational long-range goal for the one-to-oner is to see the child begin working as independently as possible, and at the same time enter more and more into the life of the church, church school, and class. Independence and belonging are goals for all who come to the school of the church. These learners are no exception.

The one-to-oners are not specialists at anything but caring. They need to know the parents and guardians well enough to be able to converse with them about the child's well-being and progress. They need to trust the child and the environment enough to let him or her try new experiences. And most of all, they need to provide comfort when a child fails and to offer a constructive suggestion about next time and perhaps propose a change of activity immediately. Because any handicap tends to slow up a child's progress, children with permanent handicaps tend to assume that normal and easy living mean the same thing. They are not as likely to see the gross blunders and errors in judgment of the other children as they are their own understandable inabilities to perform.

The one-to-oner is the child's shelter and hiding place away from home. The buddy is also at the launching pad in the church community.

HOW TO INCLUDE THE SPECIAL CHILD

There is no way to generalize about the children a church community might include in an open classroom. It is not often that you will have more than one child at a time who must depend on one-to-one supervision and activities adapted to the impairment. If you happen to be located near a resident school for the deaf or blind and many children attend, your resources are not in this book, but in the persons who teach the boys and girls day by day. When the church reaches out with a beckoning hand to the children of such a school, we also invite the teachers and leaders to counsel us, to give instructional guidance, and to worship with the congregation.

The suggestions given here for inclusion are preceded by brief profiles of children for whom they are intended. Many children will be able to perform the kinds of activities suggested, and there are many more ways to work cooperatively in spite of the handicaps. These descriptions are intended to show how to fit the abilities of a child to the needs of the group.

THE DEAF CHILD

Profile

Hamilton is ten years old and has a severe hearing loss. He goes to school with other deaf children, some of whom were born deaf. Hamilton had normal hearing until he was four years old. Then a severe infection caused a serious hearing loss. Because he had learned to talk before his hearing loss, he has more language ability than many of his day schoolmates. His speech is retarded somewhat, because it has not been developing normally since he was four. Likewise his reading and language development are on about a second-grade level. In his classroom at school he uses hearing aids and receives special instruction in speech, language, and reading. He will reach his grade level as years go on.

Hamilton did not come to church school until a deacon called on his family and explained their buddy system in use with a cerebral-palsied child. He was eager to come. When the one-to-oner met him for the first time, Hamilton shouted, "Daddy! My buddy's a boy! O-boy-o-boy! A boy!"

Learning Activities

Here are ten of the activities that Hamilton participated in at the church school's broadly graded second- through fifth-grade open classroom.

1. Hamilton painted the sky and hillside background for a mural on which other children, mostly younger than he, pasted their contributions of Jesus teaching his disciples with a crowd drawing near.

2. Hamilton's one-to-oner drew a stick-figure story of the prodigal son on write-on slides. Hamilton "read" the pictures to his buddy and later shared them with the group, telling the story himself. The small group at the clay table had made scenes for tabletop drama using clay figures to represent the father, son, older brother, and pigs. Each telling of the story reinforced the learning of the observing children.

3. Hamilton worked with various media with a degree of sensitivity. He made textured pictures with cloth, weeds, string, sandpaper, and collages conveying feelings. His favorite media were finger paint, tempera paint, and clay. His attention span was short during sharing time when the children were sitting together. While engaged in one of his projects he could sit rapt for twenty minutes.

4. During the year the class constructed a Palestinian floor village about 8′ x 10′ and a picture map of their

neighborhood on an old window shade. Hamilton helped with both projects.

5. Small groups and sometimes the whole class went on field trips related to learning center assignments. The first one was within the church and in the immediate neighborhood, so that Hamilton could become familiar with his new environment.

6. The one-to-oner brought his new camera after Christmas so that he could take colored slides of the children posing pictures in costume from the life of Christ. Hamilton began learning how to take good pictures.

7. Hamilton's buddy taught him to run the filmstrip projector, cassette player, and carousel slide projector. He learned to adjust the volume by how far he had to move the button. If it was too loud, the others would clap their hands over their ears in mock discomfort.

8. Twice during the year the opportunity arose to plant bulbs and set plants. Hamilton and his buddy used to check on the progress and report to the class. They usually took two or three others with them to the churchyard, sometimes with a magnifying glass to spot changes in texture, and other times with a ruler to detect change in size.

9. Everyone was expected to help with the maintenance of the room. Hamilton learned to clean up, put away supplies, and arrange bulletin boards and display areas for large projects.

10. Sharing periods were as visual as possible, and Hamilton's contributions always were. One day he showed them various ways of speaking in sign language, using not just his fingers but his hands in relation to head, heart, and body.

More Severe Handicap

In this classroom Hamilton's handicap was compensated for by his mobility, artistic ability, keen interest in the people and things in his environment, and the comradeship of his one-to-oner. A more profound loss of hearing dating from birth would probably have decreased his interpersonal skills and slowed further his already retarded speech, reading, language, and reasoning skills. The child who has not heard speech must learn word sense and order before reading becomes functional. Such a child suffers from lack of general information most older children and adults take for granted. Some of the children in the day school classroom with Hamilton were as much as two years behind him in the acquisition of essential general information.

THE BLIND CHILD

Profile

Jennifer is eleven years old and in sixth grade. She has been blind from birth, but she goes to school with sighted children. She spends as much time as she needs to in a resource room where a qualified teacher of the blind works with her in adapting classroom procedures and using special instructional aids. She is of normal intelligence, but because braille reading is a slower process than visual reading she is about a year behind her classmates.

At church school she works with a one-to-oner, a middle-aged woman who serves adequately as an interpreter of much of what Jennifer cannot see and has not begun to imagine. The woman wants her to be as independent as she can be in the classroom. She constructed a three-dimensional floor plan of the room with movable furniture. When a change has been made in the room arrangement she and Jennifer readjust the floor plan and then examine the room itself.

The class is broadly graded third through sixth grades. The other children react positively to Jennifer, tending at times to help her more than is necessary. Jennifer is not as much at ease with them as they are with her. She is not given to small talk or quick responses in conversations.

Before the broadly graded class was formed two years ago, Jennifer was in a conventional classroom where she sat quietly the entire time, speaking only when spoken to, and participating in minimal and nonsubstantive ways.

Learning Activities

Here are ten ways that Jennifer was involved with other class members and her work was integrated into the group's effort.

1. Stories were read and told at one center. Jennifer always spent time at that center. Geared to the children in the group who could not read well or did not like to, the center attracted younger children, generally. Jennifer was more at ease with these children than with those of her own age.

2. One of Jennifer's favorite games was "How would you end this story?" It was played at the story center. The reader stopped at the climax of the story. The listeners offered solutions and endings and then heard the ending the author proposed. Sometimes the leader brought human interest stories from newspapers and newsmagazines as a basis for the game. (This game was different from the open-ended story technique, in that the players knew that there was an ending that they would find out about eventually.)

3. In a long unit on Creation and care of the world Jennifer and the one-to-oner began a game to broaden Jennifer's experience and vocabulary. It became such a favorite with the class that they asked to play it at a party with their parents. The purpose was to assign an accurate word to a sensory experience. Jennifer had a touch box, the contents of which changed somewhat each week. When

she picked up an item she and the one-to-oner searched for a word to describe it. (Here the one-to-oner was again an interpreter for a blind person.)

She learned rough, cold, slimy, slippery, smooth but pointed, jagged, light, heavy, tepid, warm, hot. They played an old recording of sound effects once used by a church drama group and found names for the sounds taken from the natural world. Various degrees of wind and rain took up most of one side along with the crackling of fire and an explosion of dynamite. On the other side were crowd sounds of joy, disrespect, fear, awe, obedience, and command. This element in the game was easier for Jennifer than for any of the others who tried it, probably because she compensated for her blindness by cultivating her hearing.

From the smells shelf she identified wet soil, onion, cinnamon, pepper, coffee beans, a rose, a charred stick. (At the party with the parents the smells shelf was expanded to include such manufactured items as cleaning agents, kerosene, perfume, and tar.)

Tasting time allowed for a different taste each week—sweet, sour, bland, salty, nutty. Later it was combined with a fruit identification game, including such rarities as pomegranates, mangoes, and papayas.

Feeling with the mind was a vocabulary exercise aimed at becoming more forthright and articulate about feeling. "When ________________ happens, I feel ________________" was completed and discussed. Words describing feelings were sad, happy, kindly, loving, thankful, surprised, insulted, sick, relieved. The one-to-oner had a sign for the sighted children: AWFUL AND ICKY ARE NOT ALLOWED.

4. To prepare for poetry writing, the one-to-oner played an association game with Jennifer to increase her vocabulary and mental pictures. She found to her surprise that some of the associations were learned from others without regard to meaning.

She asked, "When I say *night,* what is the first word you think of?"

"Dark," Jennifer said.

"What does *dark* mean, Jennifer?"

"Oh, blue or black."

"Well, then, how does night make you feel?"

"Cool. Sleepy," she answered.

The poetry writing was a favorite activity. Poetry forms used were haiku, senru, and cinquain. The subjects began with the natural world and branched out to include relationships with others, prayer, and Christmas. These poetic forms are primarily visual to the sighted. To Jennifer they were rhythmical. She wanted them to "sound right."

5. The poetry writing led to the composing of prayers and litanies to use in class and family worship. The writing group was never more than four in number but not always the same four. Jennifer used her stylus and braille board to copy the prayers for herself. The children gathered around to watch. She couldn't hear the one-to-oner read. Finally she said: "How about if I bring the board some other time when I'm not busy? I'll teach you all how to use it." No small feat.

6. As for the singing and learning of new songs, Jennifer's memory was noticeably more active than the seeing children's. She was endowed with only average interest and ability, but the one-to-oner taught her to play the xylophone by ear or to make up tunes. She had a simple six-holed pipe she brought from home which was useful only in the key of G. She took her turn leading the group with the tambourine to keep the singing from slowing down. But what she preferred to do was sing with the whole class.

7. Jennifer was introduced to the piano the day a concert grand took up one whole side of the room on its way to die. The one-to-one showed her middle C and said that the piano was like the xylophone, except one used fingers instead of a mallet. Jennifer made up a tune to Isaiah 40:11.

Handel it was not, but she played it often enough to remember it and to teach it to one of the younger children who played it an octave above at the same time Jennifer did. It was, as she said about many things, her "favorite" verse at the moment.

8. Jennifer used the cassette player a great deal. Directions for some of the activities were recorded so that she could learn to take directions without a person doing something with her. She learned Scripture from the cassette and words to a few hymns. She recorded the children's reading of their original poetry and played it back to everyone at sharing time. She tried to record the class litany, but the words were not spoken clearly enough.

9. In a most unselfconscious moment after playing back original poetry and Scripture sung to original music, Jennifer said to her one-to-oner: "We should keep this and play it for other people. It's too good to erase." The part-time parish visitor was asked to hear it. She was so impressed that she took it on her rounds and played it to some of the shut-ins and new families joining the church.

10. The day Jennifer brought her braille equipment to sharing time she was a learning center all by herself. She was better at showing than explaining, but each child had a turn with the stylus, frame, and board. She showed them how to erase a dot and how important it was not to erase too often. Then she told them that she was writing backward, and that when she typed, everything went from left to right. One of the older boys said with awesome admiration, "Jennifer is a *genius!*"

The Dangers in Generalization

It is most important in planning learning activities for a blind child to observe that child and not to rely on generalities or, for that matter, research. In comparison to those with other handicaps, there is much more money for research and work with the blind in spite of their lesser numbers. Some of the research is contradictory. One researcher may find speech impediments more frequent than in seeing children; another will not. (One research project found superior speech among the blind!)

Another point of controversy is in the field of music. Not being able to see has very little to do with one's enjoyment, appreciation, and accomplishment in the field of music. It is probably a worthwhile area to include in any program for a blind child, but no one need expect virtuoso performance or even above-average interest from an individual in the open classroom. The reason for the inclusion of music is that hearing is a means of learning for blind children, and seeing is not.

THE CHILD WITH CEREBRAL PALSY

Profile

David is eight years old and is enrolled in a school for crippled children. He has a spastic condition in both of his legs and one arm. His mental age measured by two individually administered intelligence tests is between twelve and thirteen. He utilizes a wheelchair but may eventually be able to walk with crutches.

The family moved to the community because of the quality of the school David attends. His two older brothers attend a boarding school sixty miles away and come home each weekend. They dote on David and deliver him to the classroom at an alarming speed for a wheelchair holding such precious cargo.

The parents are determined to see that David becomes as independent as possible. His mother told the one-to-oner, a young man, "It is a lot easier to do for David instead of letting him struggle, but it's no favor to him now or later."

The open classroom at church school is for second- through fifth-graders. Since David is literally in a non-graded day school, he fits well with his chronological age group and also with older children with whom he can communicate intellectually.

There is very little he cannot do by himself that any other child might do in a seated position. The tasks of the one-to-oner are to incorporate him and his work into the efforts of the total group.

Learning Activities

Here are ten learning activities that included David in the open classroom.

1. David read stories aloud at the story center. The teachers were in the habit of putting cards at the table with questions that could be answered by reading portions of the selected books. He told each child to take a card, ask a question, give a page number, and he would do the reading. His one-to-oner had to warn him not to also answer the questions for the children.

2. David traced block letters for murals, posters, and bulletin board titles. This activity made use of both hands, his left one which he used easily and his right which was not as predictable. He was able with effort to do a neat job. Generally, one or two children sat at his feet and cut out the letters.

3. Needless to say, David was an articulate participant at planning and sharing times with the whole group. One of the teachers suggested that two young people who had been on a South American work project come to talk to them. David and two fifth-graders drew up a list of questions, gave them to the young people, and posted them for all the children to see. When the two speakers revealed that they

had slides they could show "upstairs," the one-to-oner quickly suggested that the slides be shown in the corridor outside the room. It worked well and included David.

4. The whole group at the planning time the next week phrased a letter of thanks to the young people. David volunteered to write it.

5. The one-to-oner saw quality work get lost or discarded over and over. He asked the other teachers if he might try to interest David in making a book for the class, *Best of the Open Classroom.* By year's end it contained original writing and music, paraphrases of Scripture, and colored photographs of large wall art, dramatic productions, and the mitten tree at Christmas. The one-to-oner knew the photography buff who took the pictures, but David made appointments with him by phone.

6. The puppet play was the final proof that one does not need to scamper about to participate in drama. Three older children were making papier-mâché puppets and dressing them. One of the teachers suggested several times at planning and sharing times that they might *use* the puppets to tell stories. David, with his one-to-oner, and the three puppet makers wrote a play performed on the piano bench. The script was recorded and the three puppeteers worked with the cassette recorder throughout a week and performed nobly. It was the story of Jacob and Esau with scenes all the way from getting the birthright for a bowl of stew to the reuniting years later. It took almost ten minutes, which is a lot of time for a play written by children. The audience was enthusiastic, but the puppeteers were ecstatic. In sharing time the week after, one of the teachers said that she hoped to see more puppet plays. The one-to-oner chirped: "You make the puppets, and there will be plays for them. Our story man is ready, eh, David?"

7. The neighborhood excursion was a delight. The minister broke his leg in a skiing mishap and was at home on a weekend. Ten of the boys and girls, including David,

went on an excursion out the back door of the church to the front where the congregation was entering for worship. The boys and girls asked the members to sign their names or write messages to their pastor in a composition book. Then they strode the three blocks to his home and presented the pastor with the book. When David's wheelchair cleared the steps and was pushed into the living room, the minister beckoned to him and said: "Let's see that little car of yours. I could use one of those."

8. On Epiphany Sunday a group was performing the coming of the Magi. They got to the scene with Herod at Jerusalem and decided to enlist David as Herod, because they needed his throne. It did not occur to them to ask him because this was a sitting part; it was the wheelchair they wanted. He needed no encouragement and little practice. He still had a paper crown on his head when his brothers came to get him. "Come on, King Tut," one of them said, and the little emperor was off in his mobile throne.

9. David was not fond of the housekeeping chores in the classroom, but with the encouragement and insistence of the one-to-oner, he did his share. He would feign interest in a book or bulletin board until the one-to-oner would call his bluff with, "Everybody carries freight here, old man."

10. David was expected to participate in the planning and sharing. He was not too helpful in evaluation except to say what he did not like. But in planning, he was a storehouse of ideas, however impractical. From them often came usable modifications. He cheerfully shared his work but had to be reminded that others needed time too.

Associated Disorders

There are many variations and several categories of cerebral palsy. Sometimes children have visual, hearing, and mental retardation problems. Some like David are gifted intellectually. Most cerebral palsy is detected early, and years in advance the parents and doctors are at work with treatment as well as with plans for schooling. For that reason, parents are one of the best sources of information about the child's capabilities and tolerance to a group experience with normal children.

NONFUNCTIONAL READERS

Profile

Unfortunately, this is a group profile. It is not a generalization, but a bald fact that in some upper-elementary classes in city church schools most and sometimes all of the boys and girls are nonfunctional readers. The roots of their inability to read well enough to use the skill to advantage vary from inappropriate, ineffective teaching at early ages to physical and optic abnormalities. Their attitudes toward reading and the printed material with which they are confronted reflect their belief in a no-win situation. By the time they are in sixth grade they see much of the school as an opportunity to experience failure.

It would be unfair and untrue to limit reading disability to city school and church children. In some ways the nonreading older child in a suburban or rural church is more noticeable to teachers and reading children than in the core of a large city. Surely the sense of failure is as keen, and the tolerance for it may be lower for the noncity dweller who has less company to share his misery.

The importance of a classroom climate in which a nonreading boy or girl can succeed cannot be overstated. The church has the edge on the day school in relation to its educational goals. It is not the function of the church to teach reading, useful as it would be in communicating the faith. The church's responsibility to nonreaders is to include them in significant, appropriate experiences where at long last they can come out winners, worthy and approved by themselves and others.

One of the misconceptions born of logic but not experience is that nonfunctional readers can listen to stories on tapes, spoken directions, and oral explanations to compensate for lack of reading skills. When twelve-year-olds read on a second-grade level, they hear and understand many things on that level too. The language of the neighborhood, their personal cant, may be light-years from the language of a Bible story or directions for a game.

The justified boredom of boys and girls in an environment where they do not fit is the cause of disturbing and even bizarre behavior. The educational misfits become social misfits, and without even trying, social outcasts. A sad commentary on church school classrooms.

Classroom Makeup

There are two directions to go in grouping to include older nonreaders in an open classroom. Churches have gone both ways satisfactorily. But where one direction worked, the other might first have failed.

Broadly Graded Children's Classrooms

When there are a few nonfunctional readers among reading children a broadly graded grouping of children six to eleven years of age may be a congenial place for everyone. The emphasis on small-group accomplishment rather than individual fulfillment of objectives would probably heighten the morale of the class members and almost always proves to take the limelight from the self-conscious nonreader.

In such a classroom both readers and nonreaders are found. Participants look forward to doing a good bit more than reading. The talents apart from reading skills are evident and appreciated in small, informal work groups. Eventually the boys and girls operate interdependently because of what one can do and another cannot.

One nonreader does not need, nor should the child have, an obvious one-to-oner as is necessary for the deaf, blind, and cerebral palsied. But in a class large enough for more than three small working groups, one adult leader should have the responsibility to observe and plan with nonreaders, no matter how few. With one leader in an open classroom with a five- or six-year age range, the needs of one child are often overlooked even as the child cries for help by disruption.

Intergenerational Classrooms

One church, now serving as a model to some and a curiosity to other neighboring churches, has grouped older nonreaders and readers together, with the twelve-year-olds being the youngest. Most of the projects are nonintellectual, with high participation and a strong emphasis on service to the church, individual members, and the neighborhood.

Some reading is involved in almost every activity, and many activities are repeated at various times during the year. There is, for example, regular lay participation in corporate worship, which follows Open Classroom, as it is called. Designated young persons and adults read the call to worship, the Old and New Testament lessons, and the announcements of events for the next week.

The minister is solidly behind the Open Classroom and lay leadership in worship. He tells of the first Sunday he preached at the church. The president of the congregation led a responsive reading from the hymnal. It had thirteen congregational responses, which he led with a confident, booming voice. It took twelve minutes after the new minister began timing it. Those who were reading read words one at a time without looking at phrases or sentences or anticipating them. The Lord's Prayer took no more time than it would anywhere else. It was memorized.

Now that Open Classroom is a channel for leadership, readers and nonreaders covet the position behind the center pulpit. The same call to worship is used for many weeks until it is well known by most and probably memorized. During a series of sermons the same New Testament lesson was read each Sunday.

The minister says that the emphasis is not on intellectual pursuits, but the attitude of the classroom of young people and adults is not anti-intellectual. They are using every piece of working mental machinery they have, he said. "Give me the willing unlearned to the proud stupid any day," and then he added, "and I used to be the latter."

Learning Activities

Here are ten possible ways to involve nonfunctional readers in their own learning. All have been tried and found workable somewhere. No list of them would work everywhere.

1. The spoken word, repeated often and briefly, gets translated into operative learning. A popular center with two fast friends, both poor readers, was the filmstrip and record table. Headsets and jacks made it possible to listen without disturbing others. It became obvious as two or more children came to the center that the boys were creating a disturbance by conversing with each other throughout the showing of the filmstrip. One of the teachers was a sales supervisor for a large photographic supply house and dabbler in audio-visual media. In response to the complaints of the third and fourth parties at the center, he involved the two nonreading boys in: *(a)* listening and watching the sound filmstrip they had been ignoring, *(b)* telling him what they thought were points

important enough to remember, and *(c)* cutting (yes, cutting) up the filmstrip, making slides and a new tape to go with the pictures. The new tape had one-sentence captions, and the filmstrip was reduced to half as many frames.

This teacher was not originally responsible for the educational welfare and whereabouts of nonreaders. He became the boys' buddy, not out of a buddy system, but out of the boys' preference. Those nonreaders, incidentally, were from non-English-speaking families, recently arrived in their adopted country. It would have done little good to put each one with a child who liked to read—English. That plan works in another environment. A sensitive adult who is patient with attempts to speak English and appreciative of languages other than English can be supportive of the transplanted saplings in the classroom. This man said when he assessed the difficulty, "Teach me how to say some of your words." One of the boys answered: "No, mon. We in your country. Hear?" He heard, but he hoped that by Christmas they would teach him a carol.

2. Pairing and grouping those who like to read with those who do not or cannot works well where the nonreaders are few and obvious to the teachers. Even with the pairing, it is important to include centers where reading is not essential or where printed information has preceded the work.

Curiously enough, in the church under 1, above, where even some adults could not use reading as a vehicle in their daily lives, the readers of all ages voluntarily sought out nonreaders and helped them, sometimes to excess.

With Bible study that requires reports or responses, a nonreader may appreciate being teamed with a reader. All nonreaders are not nonlisteners. Some are. Some are listeners without being articulate or even vocal in response.

In one learning center project the directions called for making a comiclike strip of the story with balloons overhead with the words of the characters in the story. A fifth grade child drew in near-stick figures a series of pictures so readily recognizable that no balloons with speech were necessary. She was listening and articulating with an active mind and a felt-nib pen. What she had needed was the initial verbal storytelling.

3. Several open classrooms have taught learners and teachers that nonreaders, even mentally retarded ones, can read numbers. Bible skills begin with finding chapter and verse and a table of contents. In a third- through sixth-grade class Bible skills were featured in a center in which everyone had to do at least one project. The nonreaders read the numbers quickly and found the page numbers quickly in the RSV Bible.

It is a thoughtful teacher who notices the progress of children doing well what they think they cannot do at all. Praise at those times is long remembered.

4. Nonreaders are not necessarily nonactors. If a story becomes well-known by telling, retelling, and dramatizing, lack of reading skills will not deter a child from taking part. In a class of sixth-graders a small group called themselves Young Players. Toward the end of the year they performed short skits of the ministry of Jesus. One of the teachers who was a spectator said after the skits were finished: "Let's *re*play a skit or two. Let's say Judas told the men that he would never betray Jesus. What would have happened?" The whole class became involved in planning a new alternative to history. One of the most imaginative contributions came from a boy with word blindness attending a special day school, "The play would be more exciting if Judas changed his mind on the stage just before he was supposed to kiss Jesus." He got the role.

5. Puppetry reinforces stories without reading. Both spectators and players profit. Nonreaders should be included in the making of puppets, the staging, and the production. In a very small class of fifth- and sixth-graders operating as a drama club, the boys and girls put on a puppet play in the corridor at the end of each of their study

units. The teacher, a former public school teacher, assessed the class as having reading abilities ranging from second grade through high school. "I'm a drama major, not a reading specialist, but I think some of these characters would have read if what they read had been more lively. At this point, though, it's hard to tell. Matt isn't interested in reading his name on a poster, and Julie—I tell you, I saw her reading the thumbtack box!" The teacher does not de-emphasize reading as a skill preceding drama, but no one who prefers not to needs to try, and much reading is done orally.

6. Familiar games adapted to objectives related to the units of study require less reading but not less thought from the players. In one open classroom where centers appeal largely to distinct age groups within the broad span of grades one through eight, the game center is popular with all age groups. The lead teacher has made them up for specific instructional reasons, and they resemble well-known games. The center is like the village well; it is where people gather. Spectators and kibitzers abound.

Who Are We? is based on charades. The stories to be acted out are typed on 3″ x 5″ cards. A team draws a card and someone reads it. The team acts out the story for the opposing team, which is given ninety seconds to guess the story. Each correct guess is worth five points. A variation on the game was done at a congregational open house. One team was to pantomime the story of Joseph up to a point they decided on, with the second team having to continue where the first stopped. It was played with two teams only. Everybody won.

We Are in a Palestinian Town and We See. . . . Describe anything from a well to a synagogue to a Roman soldier. Each team gets sixty seconds to guess and one point for a correct answer. This game was played to introduce boys and girls to a young people's picture dictionary of the Bible.

They could use the book to find items or to check on answers. Teams of two to four worked best.

We Are Going on a Missionary Journey with Paul and We Are Going to Take. . . . In this game one team of two people may challenge as unavailable what the other team decides to take. Classroom references are used to prove the point. A team who successfully challenges earns five points. An unsuccessful challenge gives the opposing team five points. If unchallenged, the article to be taken is recited by the other team, which adds one more item, and two items are recited as the first team names something else to take along.

Treasure Hunt. Send readers with nonreaders to search for clue cards and find the treasure. One hunt had a clue card in the Bible between John, chs. 12 and 13, another in a volume of *The Interpreter's Dictionary of the Bible* in the library, a third one in an adult class where players were to ask a question, get an answer, and be given the last clue. That clue led them to the kitchen, where they found edible treasure. In a hunt planned for a year-end class party, there were three groups looking for three distinct treasures. They were, as before, in the kitchen: popcorn, a popper, and oil.

7. Art activities that follow storytelling, discussions, and sound filmstrips relate to content and class activity so that nonreaders are not on the fringe of significant activity. Large cooperative murals, posters, and individual paintings and drawings all reinforce learning and sometimes reveal misconceptions. A battle scene on which David and Goliath were to be pasted for their unprecedented battle showed tanks and all manner of unidentifiable instruments of warfare. "It was a long, long, long time ago," the teacher told the artist, "before internal combustion engines, airplanes, and spaceships. They had bows and arrows, slingshots—crude instruments." The sixth-grader knew the boner was his. "The time machine got stuck," he quipped.

They named the wall scene "David and Goliath in a Twentieth-Century War."

8. Using a camera has proved fun in some groups. One older nonfunctional reader took slides with an inexpensive camera and did so well that he taught younger children in the large open classroom how to use his camera. They took pictures of activities in their classroom which were shown at a congregational meeting and described by two of the children.

9. Some music activities have been popular with those who prefer not to read. Rhythm accompaniment to some songs, composing of tunes to Scripture selections, and in one notable instance, playing the piano by ear have all been contributions from nonreaders. Making instruments can be fun too. Water glasses with different amounts of water in them can be tuned to scale and used for composing. Bells sewn to an elastic band are particularly useful around Christmas.

10. Activities that were successful and worthwhile should be repeated. Whenever a nonreading child responds enthusiastically to an activity in which he or she is learning something significant, make a note of it so that you can offer the opportunity again. No child capable of being in an open classroom with a great variety of persons should be limited to nonintellectual, peripheral, insignificant activities.

THE MENTALLY RETARDED CHILD

Profile

Mike is ten years old and has a mental age of six. He goes to school with children who have learning difficulties. The first day he was at church a returned missionary had arranged a "Learn About Lebanon" intergenerational event. There were slides, a film, curios, and a long table with art materials to occupy young children. Mike sat at the table and made clay figures for the other children. They began playing with them and asking for more. He spent a half hour "teaching" the children. On the basis of that positive experience the parents brought him the next week. He was placed in a broadly graded open classroom. He said he wanted to play with clay and was given the opportunity. He did nothing else except watch other children and show the adults what he had done each time he finished something. One of the leaders called and spoke with his father during the following week, and they arranged a conversation between the parents and the leaders of the classroom. The parents volunteered an older sister as a companion to him and then voiced a regret that she took that responsibility so often. The leaders said that they would try to find someone to be his buddy, because he so needed approval and an audience for his outgoing behavior. The one-to-oner is a ninth-grade boy who calls Mike "Partner."

Learning Activities

Here are ten things that Mike liked to do.

1. He made his own clay and modeled with it.

2. He learned to finger-paint well enough so that his designs have been used for booklet covers for the others in the class. He could use more than one color on a sheet with attractive results.

3. He painted with tempera at an easel and on a large mat of plastic on the floor.

4. He dressed up for dramatic play and delighted in what his one-to-oner called mob scenes.

5. He sang with the others and learned words and tunes easily. The one-to-oner let him record on his cassette and played it back to the other boys and girls.

6. He drew on the chalkboard.

7. He listened to stories over and over again.

8. He watched a sound filmstrip every Sunday, many times the same brief filmslip made of crayon drawings by children.

9. He helped the one-to-oner tell a story to the whole group by placing flannel-backed figures on the flannel board. He told a story like that to his one-to-oner each week.

10. He cleaned up and put art materials away. He was fastidious.

Ten is an arbitrary number of activities to list in each of these categories. It was chosen to guard against the generalities of "several," "many," and "few." It is a large enough number to encourage those leaders looking at the potentials of open classroom organization to include all those children for whom it would be a positive experience. When a classroom is organized around openness, its spirit can reflect that openness to those unaccustomed to it.

6 Improving What Already Works

Until you have tried openness in the classroom, you disbelieve those who say they get better at planning, classroom management, and evaluation as they continue. They also tell you that discipline problems virtually disappear. One of the reasons for that, of course, is the great number of options a child has for getting work done. And another is that the planning allows for individual differences, preferences, and abilities.

SHIFTING GEARS

When children are involved in planning and evaluation, moving from one kind of openness to another is not jarring. If you have used contracts (described in Chapter 2) for several months and shift to a broadly graded grouping with group objectives, the amount of preplanning may be less and the class's planning and weekly preparation may take more time.

If you interrupt learning center education with observable individual outcomes in order to have a seasonal intergenerational event, the boys and girls should be able to help in the planning by stating their preferences of learning activities. Older elementary children sometimes serve on planning committees for intergenerational events.

No matter what form of openness you choose, expect it to keep changing as you and the other participants change. The absence of one enthusiast can make a difference in the disposition of the group at a given session. In one of the week-long resident leadership schools a fourth-grade girl was eager to try everything in the broadly graded open classroom. She nearly succeeded and raised the level of participation of many others as well. On Thursday afternoon she got sick and did not attend on Friday. On Saturday morning before they dismantled the work centers, the evaluation session was held.

"It wasn't as much fun yesterday," a second-grade boy commented.

"Why was that?" a teacher asked.

"I didn't know what to do, I guess."

"Boys and girls get pretty tired at these schools," another teacher reasoned.

"I got sick," the enthusiast said. "I didn't even want to come I was so sick."

"That's why Jimmy didn't have fun, I bet," another child spoke up. "Betty makes us want to try everything, and when she wasn't here, we just hung around."

Similar changes come with the shifting of leadership. Although all the leaders need not be at each session, some dependable, familiar persons should continue throughout the year. The less attention you pay to achievement of objectives, completion of work, and high expectations in concept development, the easier shifting of leadership becomes. Where the quality of education is high, the leadership is stable, changing only for intergenerational events and workshops. The number of occasional helpers in both children's classes and intergenerational programs should change as the curriculum changes. Herein lies your first well of leaders to be prepared for the future.

GETTING LEADERSHIP

The word about open classrooms gets around, and the news varies from place to place. Often, because the program is new to the church, people regard the teachers as great innovators and feel that they could not possibly qualify as teachers. Sometimes they are right.

In one church where the "open" classroom was in fact quite closed, teachers operated on a one-to-one basis with each child's program different from the others. They spent about thirty hours planning each unit and a few hours in assessment and adaptation each week. When one of the prime movers could not teach for a year, the program had to be modified in order to get leadership. Even if a person who could spend that amount of time was found, it would be highly unlikely that the quality of the planning would produce the results of the previous teachers. It does little good to expect a worthwhile program from leadership that cannot determine what is worthwhile and what is not.

INFORMING THE CONGREGATION

One of the advantages of open education programs is the visibility of the change. More work gets done, much of which can be shared with the congregation. In two churches in one small community children painted murals on the walls outside their classrooms. In the public school classroom the next day one child reported on the progress of the mural that was changing the basement decor.

"We're doing one at our church too," her classmate told the teacher. "It's about Palestine." Their teacher was clearly among the nonbelieving until the weekly newspaper published pictures of the completed projects and described the open classrooms. Every Sunday, for weeks, visitors came to observe the mural in one of the churches. One Sunday it was painted over. The next Sunday a new one was begun, creating more curiosity.

An open classroom in a very large church displays its work two or three times a year in an entryway that is roughly 20′ x 20′. Artwork, models, box scenes, and puppets are on walls and tables. At one display child guides in Biblical costume were showing a few adults in a spontaneous dramatization what a synagogue school was like.

In that church the word got around that teaching in the open classroom is worth it and fun. The leaders constantly involved helpers from the congregation for short-term responsibilities. When it came time to replace hardy perennials, they had knowledge of the kinds of help they might get from a good many individuals. People were hardly standing in line to volunteer, but from its inception, the classroom has continued to have an adequate staff and cooperative assistants.

NURTURING THE RECRUITS

As soon as vacancies are known, the hunt for replacements should begin so that the rookies can visit, attend a planning meeting, and be short-term helpers. Everyone, no matter how well equipped, needs orientation in open classroom procedures. No two organizational patterns turn out to be the same in goals, expectations of leaders and learners, and schedule.

Even in areas where churches have admittedly adopted the open classroom procedures of one model church, what has come to be is an open classroom in each church unlike any other. As one of the pioneers tells church school teachers who want to know how to do it *right:* "There are many right ways; also some wrong ones. One of the wrong ones is thinking yours is the only right way."

More important than any other attribute of every smoothly running open classroom nurturing new recruits is thoughtfulness. Where this prevails the neophyte is not afraid to ask questions, make suggestions, and take responsibility. In some of the classrooms, new leaders are surprised to see children instructing children. And in still others, children instruct leaders.

One of the last acquired skills of new leaders is observation of how children learn. Exposure to the planning, execution, and teacher-learner evaluation is the place to start learning. When the class is small or where leaders have certain children as their responsibility, observation skills soon come to the point of usefulness.

In a well-designed broadly graded open classroom a new leader reported that "everyone seemed to have such fun." It was not until her first evaluation session with leaders and children that she discovered that every child had a logbook in which he or she or a teacher had recorded the work they had accomplished, with whom they worked, and how they liked the results. She had not seen the books. She had not noticed the kinds of relationships the children had with the adults. She had not been aware of what work was finished and what was left undone. "There was so much going on and so much to look at, I didn't see details," she said.

Involvement is the secret to successful orientation. As the children learn by doing, so do the teachers. In a church with learning centers in small rooms of two grades each, two new teachers were being oriented for grades 3–4 and 5–6. The class was to terminate for summer program on Pentecost Sunday and resume after Labor Day. At the coffee hour the two were talking to a member of the Christian education committee. "I can hardly wait until fall," one told him. "It's such a difference from what I knew."

The other woman said: "I feel that way too. I'm not in the driver's seat. The kids are. We furnish the maps and the travel counsel. They decide which place to go."

When the member reported the comments to the committee, the chairman confessed that he was most unimpressed with the first year of the learning center approach. "Whenever I looked in those rooms there were children lying on their stomachs reading and men and women sitting on the floor talking to kids or playing games. Now I have to admit it's a valid educational program."

The minister, who had been both leader and advocate of the program, sighed. "George, I told you learning centers aren't for everyone and everything. But they sure are for us and our purposes. We have never had better morale in the whole church or," he added, "better informed leadership, including you."

WORKING WITH OTHER CHURCHES

The word spreads to other churches and often the naïve request comes, "Come to our teachers' meeting and tell us how to have an open classroom." The answer to that probably should be, "Come to our church and watch."

A minister who became involved in helping other churches begin open classrooms says in retrospect that he would not again attend teachers' meetings and talk. "The children learn by doing not by listening to a teacher tell them what works."

What he would do instead he thought of too late. He would run a weekend school over the period of a unit in which observation, lab experience, seminar, and evaluation would all be a part. "They have to see it, be in it, plan for it, and evaluate it before they are ready to start their own classroom." He said he would contract with the participants, and if too many faulted, he would not continue. "They have to want to work to make this a viable educational alternative to whatever it is they're doing."

Nearby churches should always be free to call and invite themselves to visit. If space is limited in a learning center classroom with observable outcomes and contracted work, the number of visitors needs to be limited. That is why visitors should call beforehand and make an appointment.

In a broadly graded classroom with activity centers or centers with group objectives, the room is generally large enough to accommodate roving visitors. It is still a good idea to call ahead, because visitors should see a normal session, not a special adaptation.

If you are the one receiving a call from another church, suggest that the teachers come to a planning meeting so that some of the leaders get a look at part of the iceberg under the water.

Pooling Resources

Many communities, large and small, have resource centers with a variety of materials and equipment. Some of the large city centers or regional centers have films as well as filmstrips, slide sets, and records. Some share projectors of several kinds, tape recorders, and screens. More centers are on a smaller scale and pool what member churches have and buy new materials with pooled contributions. Books, records, and filmstrips are the staples of such resource centers. It is best to cooperate interdenominationally and with churches adapting diverse materials, so that everyone does not require the same book or filmstrip on the same Sunday.

Pooling People

A fairly recent phenomenon in church education is the independent consultant who, for a price, will conduct workshops and offer consultative services. Some churches can afford to entertain a consultant for a one-day, two-day, or one-week workshop. Most cannot.

As a consequence, local councils of churches, denominational judicatories, and informally connected congregations join forces to hold workshops on their areas of weakness. The independent consultant, to be worth the money spent, should be informed about what the cooperating churches want and should give the inquiring churches a list of the services he or she offers.

Open education is one area that might be explored. Learning center classrooms with observable outcomes is a more precise area. Intergenerational educational models is precise too. Teacher competence is general. Functions and competencies for leaders in open education models is a more precise request. The more specific the request, the more a consortium gets for its money. Denominational judicatory headquarters know of independent consultants, their qualifications, and their whereabouts.

KEEPING RECORDS

Learning how to become more and more adept at operating an open classroom of any design is a good bit like becoming a gourmet cook. You discover your strengths, you invent out of necessity and sometimes near-failure, and you approach any new problem with a history of having done well.

You can rely on your memory, if you have a good one, for the varieties of art activities, poetic forms, and review games you have found useful. Most of us find ourselves using the same ideas over and over, and no matter how masterful we are at putting the concoction together, it can become tiresome.

Like the gourmet, the leader of an open classroom should *write down* what made a particular creation escape the ordinary. Several teams of teachers in open classrooms have developed logs containing plans, copies of learners' work, descriptions of activities, recipes that really work for clay and finger paint, ideas borrowed from others but still unused, and ever-changing lists of books, filmstrips, and records. With curriculum materials on a two-year cycle, the plans can be used again with far less effort than the first time when the major adaptation to openness had to be made. Furthermore, everything useful is in one place.

A couple who taught a fairly small group of third- and fourth-graders in an atmosphere of openness were working with new teachers, using what they referred to as a scrapbook. They even had colored pictures of the children's work. One of the student teachers asked how she could get hold of a book like that, and the man replied, "Start now."

The distinctive feature of a collection made by a group of three organizers and several off-and-on assistants of a broadly graded classroom was organization of art activities into categories. One heading was "Telling the Story with Art." There were directions for painted, textured, and paste-on murals, a shoe-box movie, an accordion cardboard class book, a clothesline art story, a write-on filmstrip, a Japanese picture box, and more. The purpose of each activity was the same, but with a record like that, the danger of repeating the same one over and over is minimal.

"Remember," said an old hand to a teacher who was afraid she would run out of ideas, "there are twenty-one ballet steps and only seven basics. Think what the combinations can produce."

THE SAMPLER

At a week-long resident school one of the individual assignments was to begin a resource book, which would be continued after the student teachers went home. The participants soon learned that cooperative work made better individual books just as it makes better open classroom planning. Every book that went home with a student was unlike every other, but each shared many things from the others.

Recipes

A woman who had taught in conventional classrooms for years donated and demonstrated her recipes for salt-and-flour clay and finger paint. "There are other ways to make these materials," she wrote, "but these recipes are the best and the hardest to find."

Clay

3 parts flour
3 parts salt
1 teaspoon powdered alum

Combine. Add water gradually until the dough is soft and pliable. If you like colored clay, add food coloring to the water before mixing. It won't hurt a child to eat this, but no one would want to.

Finger Paint

½ cup cornstarch
½ cup cold water
3½ cups boiling water
2 tablespoons glycerin
oil of cloves

Add the cold water to the cornstarch gradually, stirring constantly until smooth. Add boiling water slowly and cook until clear. Cool. Stir in glycerin and a few drops of oil of cloves. Add either liquid poster paints or powdered tempera for color as you need it. Keep leftover paint in the refrigerator.

Poetry Forms

The contributor and compiler of the three forms of structured nonrhyming poetry found them to be popular with third- through sixth-graders. She believes that the more poetry they have read to them, the better poetry children write.

Haiku and Senru

Haiku and senru are Japanese forms. They are exactly alike in form. They differ in function. Haiku presents a single thought related to nature. Senru is a single thought on any subject. The formula is:

Line 1: 5 syllables
Line 2: 7 syllables
Line 3: 5 syllables

Spring came in April
Later than ever before
Welcome, tardy spring!

Cinquain

Though cinquain is a French word meaning "group of five," this poetic form is of American origin. The formula is:

Line 1: 2 syllables, a title
Line 2: 4 syllables, describing the title
Line 3: 6 syllables, action of the title

Line 4: 8 syllables, feeling about the title
Line 5: 2 syllables, synonym of title

Jesus
Man for others
Went about doing good.
How I wish I could have been there.
Savior.

Younger children are able to use a cinquain adaptation before they understand syllables. Here is the formula:

Line 1: 1 word as title
Line 2: 2 words about title
Line 3: 3 words of action of title
Line 4: 4 words of feeling
Line 5: 1 word synonymous with title

Crayons

The maligned crayon had its day in the sun with a demonstration from a minister who said he had once gone to "coloring school," an all-day workshop put on by a crayon company. The first thing he did was peel the crayons so that the whole surface of the crayon could be used. Then he showed how the surface under the drawing paper could be used to artistic advantage. He put the paper on a sand-finished wall and colored a green-and-yellow meadow. He used corrugated paper, screen, and sandpaper as undersurfaces as well. He showed how to use the side of a crayon for a brush technique and then introduced two art forms.

Crayon Etching

Use cardboard no bigger than 5″ x 7″ the first time. Draw a scribble picture and fill in the design with a variety of bright-colored crayons applied heavily. Then color the whole surface with a black crayon. A picture may be drawn on this colored surface by scratching the surface with a pointed object. Different effects are produced by the use of scissors points, a big needle, toothpicks, and a comb. The pictures are novelties but can convey feeling that other art forms cannot.

Crayon Resist

Draw a picture with light-colored crayons applied heavily. Brush the entire picture with india ink or a thick wash of watercolor. Let it dry about five minutes, and then hold the paper under cold running water until the drawing shows. Spread the drawing on newspapers to dry.

Chalk

The minister who had gone to "coloring school" also contributed his knowledge of chalk as a classroom medium. He used colored chalk on wet manila paper, holding it sometimes like a pencil but mostly flat on its side and broken to a two-inch length.

He used wet chalk on dry paper, holding the chalk like a pencil and making outlined figures. Then he painted over the drawing quickly with thin watercolor creating a resist effect.

He also demonstrated buttermilk painting with chalk. He poured the liquid on manila paper and spread it around with his fingers. As he began drawing with chalk, the colors and texture were vibrant. The smell was offensive to some of the spectators, but it was gone completely by the time the picture dried. (It is that kind of reaction which should be recorded in a log, so that a planner is warned of negative responses.)

Story Game

Two student teachers adapted a game in order to introduce the details of a story rather than to review them as all the other classroom games did. They felt the need to teach children Bible stories that are not generally in the mainstream of church school curriculum but are worth knowing. They listed Noah, the tower of Babel, David and Goliath, Daniel in the lion's den, and the three men in the fiery furnace. Their game is based on the last-named story.

Make out twelve 3″ x 5″ cards as printed below. Each player chooses one card in turn and does as directed. Each keeps his or her own score, or one scorekeeper can keep a record on a chalkboard. Everyone starts with 100.

Card No. 1: Nebuchadnezzar was the king who took the Jews from Jerusalem to Babylon.

All those who have an N in their name add 5 points.

Card No. 2: One day the king decided to make a golden idol for everyone to worship.

Subtract 10 points from everyone's score.

Card No. 3: All the important people were called to stand before the idol.

Subtract 5 points from your score. Everyone else remains the same.

Card No. 4: The king's messenger told the people: "Fall down and worship the idol. All of you!"

Subtract 10 points from your score.

Card No. 5: Three Jewish men would not fall down. Their names were Shadrach, Meshach, and Abednego.

Give 5 points each to three persons of your choice. Take none for yourself.

Card No. 6: The king was angry. "If you do not fall down before the idol, you will be thrown into a burning furnace!" he shouted. "And who is the god that will save you then?"

Subtract or add to your score to make it 75.

Card No. 7: "Our God is able to save us," Shadrach, Meshach, and Abednego answered. "But even if he does not, we will not worship the golden image."

All those who have S, M, or A in their names add ten points.

Card No. 8: Nebuchadnezzar was furious. He ordered the furnaces heated up seven times hotter than usual. The three Jews were tied and thrown into the furnace. The soldiers who threw them in died of the heat.

All those who have shoestrings in their shoes get 5 points.

Card No. 9: The king came to look into the furnace. He was astonished. "Did we not cast *three* bound men into the furnace?" he cried out. "I see *four* men loose, and the fourth looks like a son of the gods."

Give yourself 10 points and three other people 20.

Card No. 10: Nebuchadnezzar came near the door of the fiery furnace and called, "Shadrach, Meshach, and Abednego, servants of the Most High God, come here!"

Give yourself 20 points.

Card No. 11: The three men came forward. Their hair was not singed. Their clothes were not burned, and there was no smell of fire or smoke about them.

Give three persons 15 points. Give yourself the same.

Card No. 12: The king said, "Blessed is your God who sent his angel to save you. You trusted no other god and refused to serve any except your own God."

All double their scores.

Use of the Tape Recorder

The instructor contributed his list of uses of the cassette recorder and player, a piece of equipment he considers essential to his classroom.

1. A story that is told to the group as basic to the introduction of a unit, he also tapes for absentees. At the beginning of the second session of a unit a teacher meets with those who were absent for the first session to explain the work of the centers. Then the absentees listen to the tape of the story.

2. Directions for Bible skill exercises and games are taped. He says on the tape: "Turn off the recorder while you examine the table of contents and find Matthew." A work sheet accompanies the tape. When a child shows one of the teachers the completed work sheet, the teacher okays it or says, "Listen to the first part of the tape again."

3. Children who have been absent can learn songs from a tape. If the song is an uncomplicated folk song, it is taped with someone singing it alone and then with the whole group. If it is a hymn requiring some introduction, the teacher tapes the assembly period in which the hymn is introduced. A work sheet with words is available for the learners.

4. Directions for small-group games have been put on tape even though the written directions accompany the game. Some boys and girls listen more accurately than they read. Many an argument has been settled by playing the tape.

5. A tape was made at a book fair the instructor attended. He talked to an illustrator and an author about the kinds of things the boys and girls like to read about, and asked where they got their ideas for pictures and prose. He did the tape in order to show interview techniques so that interview projects would be chosen more often than they were.

6. An interview was planned and taped by a single

sixth-grade girl. The church was without a pastor, and she interviewed the pulpit committee chairman. She asked bald questions and received clear answers. The instructor said it was a better interview than his.

7. They always tape puppet plays so that they can practice the action and make it as explicit as possible. No attention needs to be given to remembering lines, and two or three children are capable of doing the whole project. The spectators are always enthusiastic about these plays.

8. When the instructor went to the hospital with viral pneumonia one of the other teachers suggested that they write a hasty get-well letter on a roll of shelf paper. They liked the idea, but they were so accustomed to the divided labor of the open classroom that while the letter was being designed a tape was made of greetings, trite jokes, and sounds of pandemonium. Two boys sang an "original premiere performance" of a dreadful lay to the tune of "Blest Be the Tie That Binds."

> "We're sorry that you are in bed.
> We wish we could be there instead.
> And if you survive
> To get out of that dive,
> We'll know you are living not dead."

9. For two weeks a French-speaking child, open-mouthed but silent, visited the classroom. By the second session the instructor had a story taped in French and a filmstrip with a French script that the child heard with a headset. The child, who was accustomed to being in limbo, was amused and diverted. His parents, who tutored him on their cross-country jaunt for their company, were effusive in their praise of the young man's thoughtfulness.

10. One of the permanent centers is "Service." In each unit's work one category is service. It is not related to content, but it is a part of the life of the church. Some tasks

are simple: "Find out from the parish visitor the name and address of one shut-in. Send a card saying, 'I am thinking of you.' " One of the tasks is "Record a tape that would be enjoyed by the people Mr. Roulston visits at Quiet Acres. Check with a teacher before you begin." The same two boys who wrote the dirge in No. 8 recorded children's singing in the nursery, the kindergarten and first grade, and the open classroom. And no gothic doggerel.

LAST WORDS

The instructor of the student teachers who contributed to their community log is not alone in his energetic espousal of open classroom techniques and his zeal for sharing them with others. Zeal and a constant push to improve what is already working is characteristic of the leadership of open education in the church. With few exceptions they were competent teachers in conventional classrooms and operated in an open manner there without the advantage of an open organization. They bring valuable experience to the open classrooms in which they teach and to the student teachers who learn from them.

"I'm going over to the dime store to get a notebook for my open classroom scrapbook," an eager student teacher told her mentor. "What kind is the best?"

"One you can add to indefinitely," her instructor told her. And she meant it.

That is open education.